Minute Meditations™ *for* Busy Moms

EMILIE BARNES

HARVEST HOUSE PUBLISHERS
Eugene, Oregon 97402

Cover by Terry Dugan Design, Minneapolis, Minnesota

MINUTE MEDITATIONS™ FOR BUSY MOMS
Copyright © 2002 by Emilie Barnes
Published by Harvest House Publishers
Eugene, Oregon 97402

Library of Congress Cataloging-in-Publication Data
Barnes, Emilie.
    Minute meditations for busy moms / Emilie Barnes
        p. cm.
    ISBN 0-7369-0831-5
    1. Mothers—Prayer-books and devotions—English. I. Title.

BV4847 .B36 2002
242'.6431—dc21   2001038513

Printed in the United States of America.

03 04 05 06 07 / BC-MS / 10 9 8 7 6 5 4 3

Dedication

The following meditations are dedicated to all you busy moms who are struggling to maintain balance in your lives. I remember what it's like to have to juggle the many ceaseless demands that require the special touch that only Mom can provide.

For me, those wonderful days are now past. I wish they had never left, but they have. And one thing I have learned about life is that we must be willing to enjoy our memories of the past, but always continue to look to the future.

Someone once wrote:

"Yesterday is history,
tomorrow is a mystery,
today is God's gift,
that's why we call it the present."

As you read these meditations, may you truly look upon them as a gift from me to you. Each one has been written from my life's experiences and is passed on to you, the reader, as wisdom. As you read each selection, my prayer is that you will think about what you've read, act upon it, and make it part of your life. I also hope that you'll freely share the wisdom you gain with another busy mom and thus refresh her soul.

James says to be "doers of the word, and not merely hearers" (James 1:22). Act upon each challenge so that you begin to understand how God fits into this whole experience called motherhood. In so doing, may you become a richer, more relaxed, balanced, purposeful, and loving woman.

—*Emilie Barnes*

A Note from Emilie

I've written this devotional book for every busy mom who wants to get in touch with her Lord and her life. Each meditation is designed to take such a short time from your busy day that you'll still have time to study God's Word, where you'll find help and direction for your everyday life.

Another unique feature of this book is that you don't have to start at the beginning. You can skip around and choose the reading that seems most suited for the day ahead. At the top of each page you will see three boxes. Each time you read a meditation, put a check mark in one of the boxes. In this way you can keep track of those selections that have been previously read.

Also, the prayer accompanying each reading is to help you get started. Once you feel comfortable creating your own conversation with God, I would encourage you to pray with your own words. Some women I know choose to journal their prayers as a way to record their time spent with the Lord. You also might find that practice useful.

Each meditation closes with a recommended action that can help busy moms implement what they've read into their daily life. Some of the suggestions are practical, others are for pure fun—but all are designed to help make being a mom more enjoyable.

And after all, that's what God intends for mothers— a life of joy in nurturing the wonderful gifts He's given us in our children.

Good News
Before Bad News

All Scripture is inspired by God and profitable for teaching, for reproof, for correction, for training in righteousness; so that the man of God may be adequate, equipped for every good work.

—2 TIMOTHY 3:16-17

*S*ome days I wake up and reach for the morning paper or turn on the radio to catch the latest newscast. After all, it's important to be well informed about world events. But after a few short days of this, I'm reminded of a saying that I once heard, *Read the Good News before you read the bad news.*

That's absolutely right. Why would any busy mother, already carrying the important responsibilities of her family, want to start the day off with the bad news that always seems to make the biggest headlines before she reads the Good News of Scripture?

Over the years I've made it a point to start off each day by reading and thinking about God's Word. When the children were young, I set the alarm 30 minutes before the rest of the family's wake-up call so I could start the day off right. This practice seemed to energize my day as a mother and set me heading in the right direction. On days when I skipped my time with the Lord, I often encountered frustration and lack of focus. I seemed to move along from one small crisis to the next, without the peace that only comes as a result of time spent alone with God.

Recently I came across a magazine article that caught my eye and heart. It was a story about John Stott, the 80-year-old renowned theologian and author of many books. Dr. Stott is a man of God who wields worldwide influence in the evangelical community. I suspect part of his success is due to his daily practice of beginning each morning at 5 A.M. with this Trinitarian Prayer:

> Good morning, heavenly Father; good morning, Lord Jesus; good morning, Holy Spirit. Heavenly Father, I worship you as the Creator and Sustainer of the universe. Lord Jesus, I worship you, Savior and Lord of the world. Holy Spirit, I worship you, Sanctifier of the people of God. Glory to the Father, and to the Son, and to the Holy Spirit. As it was in the beginning, is now, and will be forever. Amen.
>
> Heavenly Father, I pray that I may live this day in your presence and please you more and more. Lord Jesus, I pray that this day I may take up my cross and follow you. Holy Spirit, I pray that this day you will fill me with yourself and cause your fruit to ripen in my life: love, joy, peace, patience, kindness, goodness, faithfulness, gentleness, and self-control. Holy, blessed, and glorious Trinity, three persons in one God, have mercy upon me. Amen.[1]

Each morning after reading and meditating prayerfully over three chapters of Scripture, Dr. Stott pulls out his prayer notebook and prays for his friends, family, ministries, and even strangers for whom he has a burden.

Here is a man who has dedicated his life to knowing God in a personal way. Because of his dedication and commitment to godliness he lives a rich and balanced life.

Would that I could grasp just a glimpse of his modeling for my life. Here is a man who definitely believes in reading the Good News before he reads the bad news.

And though you and I may never have the worldwide influence Dr. Stott has, we *do* have a profound influence on the homes we create for our family. We need all the strength God can give us.

Prayer

Father God, just hearing about John Stott's commitment to You energizes my commitment to You. My desire is to know You as he does. Help me realize the full benefits of being Your child every day. Be my strength, O God. Amen.

Action

Prayerfully read John Stott's Trinitarian Prayer each day for one month. Also, as a prayer aid, create your own prayer notebook and divide it into four sections: friends, family, ministries, and strangers. Write the names of your various acquaintances under each of these headings and pray for them on a regular schedule.

Creating a prayer journal helps us focus our prayers. Often, without such a journal or prayer list, we pray randomly and without purpose.

When you pray for your children, list each one individually. Every child is different and has different needs.

"In Everything" Not "For Everything"

In everything give thanks;
for this is the will of God in Christ Jesus for you.
—1 THESSALONIANS 5:18 (NKJV)

*L*ast evening we received two telephone calls that really test this verse. One was regarding a 15-year-old boy who had just been hospitalized to begin a grueling chemotherapy regimen to combat his newly diagnosed cancer.

The next call was regarding a mother who went in for a midlife hysterectomy. The doctors, in performing a routine biopsy, discovered cervical cancer.

How do we say "Thank You God" for tragedies and sudden crises that threaten to destroy our world? I struggled with this question until I realized that this passage says, "*in* everything, not *for* everything."

"In everything" is not the same as "for everything." We don't give thanks for evil or for its tragic results. And at some time or another, we all come face to face with evil or an unexpected crisis that threatens us or our family. At such times, no mother can be thankful for the evil that threatens her loved ones, but she can and must be thankful to the God who oversees all that comes our way.

Even in the midst of our pain, God is always at work. We can remain grateful throughout our ordeal because we live in Jesus Christ and because we know that God cares for us even more than we care for our own children. God is the only perfect parent—and in Him, we find refuge in the day of trouble. Through every circumstance that comes our way, God continues to transform us into the image of His Son.

Matthew Henry, the well-known Bible commentator, made the following entry in his diary after he had been robbed:

> Let me be thankful—first, because I was never robbed before; second, because although they took my wallet, they did not take my life; third, because although they took my all, it was not much; and fourth, because it was I who was robbed, not I who robbed.

Here is a man who knew how to make lemonade out of a lemon. Here is a man who could give thanks *in* everything.

The art of successful living is to seek out thankfulness in all of life's events—to see meaning in every challenge and trust that God will work every adversity to our ultimate good.

It's like the mom who opened the door to her young son's bedroom and saw the boy digging in a large pile of manure. The mother asked, "What on earth are you doing?"

Without a pause the boy replied, "Mommy, with all this manure there's got to be a pony in here somewhere!"

Prayer
Father God, I pray today that Your will will be done in my life. Help me give thanks "in everything." Help me to look closely to see the good in all that You do. Amen.

Action
As you go through your day, resolve to give thanks "in everything."

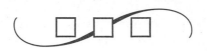

Have Sunbeams in Your Hands

He showed them his hands...

—LUKE 24:40 (NIV)

*D*o you take your hands—the hands of a hardworking mother—for granted? Are your fingers and thumbs just ten appendages about which you barely give a thought until the slightest injury prevents you from lifting, tying, opening, squeezing, or doing any of the myriad tasks a mom does daily?

Like us, Jesus had hands. And also like us, Jesus used His hands to bless others, to minister healing and comfort. Although His carpenter's hands were strong and rough, He used them as tools of blessing. With them, He held the children who came to Him. With them, He healed the sick. And in John 10:28 He gives us a picture of the security we have in His saving hand: "I give them eternal life, and they shall never perish; no one can snatch them out of my hand" (NIV). It was by His hands that Jesus hung on the cross, spilling blood that paid the price for our sins.

The hands of those I meet often speak louder than their words. I have met people so empty of joy that when I clasped their frosty fingertips it seemed as if I were shaking hands with a northeast storm. There are others whose hands have sunbeams in them, so that their grasp warms my heart. In the touch of a child's hands especially, there is as much sunshine as there is in a loving glance from my dearest friend.

Prayer

Father God, let me never take for granted the precious hands You have given me at birth. When I touch people, I want them to feel Your sunshine through my hands. Use my hands today to bless others and especially my children. Amen.

Action

Give thanks to God for your hands.

Don't Let Go

He will walk hand in hand with you
Through the paths of this new day—
You will feel the warmth of His gentle grip
And your feet will not go astray…
For He'll be at your side to expertly guide
Or support when weakened or tired,
And when trouble you meet, He will lift your feet
And carry you over the mire
If you stumble or fall, He will hear your call
And immediate comfort you'll know,
So reach out today for the Savior's strong hand—
It is you, not HE, that lets go!

—ELIZABETH PEARSON

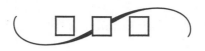

I Pledge You My Troth

...it is required of stewards that one be found trustworthy.
—1 CORINTHIANS 4:2

> As rowers in a boat turn their backs to the shore and trust to the man at the helm, whose eye is fixed upon it; so should we proceed in duty through life—turn our backs from our anxious cares for the future, and leave the guidance of them all to God, who guides the helm.[2]

In the old wedding ceremonies there was a wonderful phrase that read, "I pledge thee my troth." I often wondered, "What's a troth? Something to drink out of?"

In looking the word up, I discovered that it originally meant a pledge to be true, faithful, loyal, and honest. It can also mean trust, reliability, and integrity in marriage. It's what we would call "fidelity" today. "Fidelity" is the word we use when we want to show that we will be faithful in marriage.

We exhibit fidelity, our troth, when we pour our energy into making our marriage function as God envisions it. Daily, we're to live out what we promised to God at the altar. We also show our fidelity by building a fence around our marriage to protect our relationship from the enemy who would like to come in and destroy what God put together.

At times that fence might shut out sports, trips, TV, music, hobbies, even on occasion our children or church activities. We are not to let *anything* drain us of our energy to fulfill our part in a healthy marriage. As mothers, the maintenance of a happy marriage is critical to the security and happiness of our children. Stable families are more likely to produce stable, well-adjusted children. A mother's commitment to the father of her children is one of the best investments she can make for the future of her children.

Fidelity is a calling to be faithful in every area of marriage. One of the chief drains on our maternal energy is our participation in otherwise fine activities that end up robbing us of the time and energy we need to succeed as mothers and wives.

Are there activities in your life—a job, a club, a volunteer position, a church duty—that are taking you away from your main responsibility, that of a mother to your children and a faithful wife to your husband? If so you must reevaluate those time robbers and eliminate or scale back as necessary.

Prayer

Father God, let me examine my activities to see if any of them are robbing me from being the best mother and wife that I can be. Give me the courage to make some hard decisions. Amen.

Action

Be willing to make some hard decisions today—and follow through.

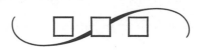

The Account of My Tears

You have taken account of my wanderings;
put my tears in Your bottle. Are they not in Your book?
—Psalm 56:8

$\mathcal{D}$avid was amazed that God was attentive to every detail of his life—even down to the awareness of the tears he shed. It truly *is* amazing to think that our God is so intimately concerned for us that He not only notices our tears but saves them in His bottle as jewels.

We're also given the promise that "they that sow in tears shall reap in joy" (Psalm 126:5 KJV). And as a mother, you *will* sow tears—many tears. Some will be tears of joy as your children move through the various landmarks of life—the first steps, the first day of school, the first romantic crush, graduation day, marriage....

But some tears will be those of pain—the first bruised knee, the first hurtful words hurled your way as your child speaks his or her mind...and the first breakup of that romantic crush that brought happiness to your child. Though some of these crises seem minor, they are major to the person involved.

Our grandson Chad called the other evening, and his heart was crushed and his tears had flowed because his girlfriend had called and said she needed "space." I could tell from his voice that he was so hurt. Because of his tears,

I too had tears for his heartbreak, and I believe in some real way, God was shedding tears for my 16-year-old grandson.

Countless nights through the years my pillowcase has been stained with tears for my children. And each time, I've claimed Psalm 30:5: "Weeping may last for the night, but a shout of joy comes in the morning."

Yes, as mothers, there will be many nights when you go to bed with a heavy heart and tears in your eyes. At such times allow yourself to fall asleep meditating on this healing verse. Then awake to joy—God is in control!

> We must not hope to be mowers,
> And to gather the ripe gold ears,
> Unless we have first been sowers
> And watered the furrows with tears.
> It is not just as we take it,
> This mystical world of ours,
> Life's field will yield as we make it
> A harvest of thorns or of flowers.
> —JOHANN WOLFGANG VON GOETHE

Prayer

Father God, You are with me every time I shed a tear, for whatever reason; I'm also confident that You are crying when I cry. We both know that there will be a shout of joy in the morning. I praise You, O Lord. Amen.

Action

Know that when you cry, God cries along with you.

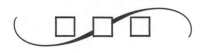

Live Life on Purpose

*Whether, then, you eat or drink or whatever you do,
do all to the glory of God.*

—1 Corinthians 10:31

Have you ever been challenged to live life *on purpose*? If not, I so challenge you now. Especially your life as a mother. God has plans for your children—and for you. It's not His will that we coast through life casually and aimlessly. Life's far too short for that.

God has placed us here on earth for a reason. And when we discover that reason and live our life to that godly end, we find true satisfaction.

In my life I've been fortunate to meet a lot of wonderful people. All walks of life, all colors, all denominations—some with no denominations. But the ones I count the most successful are those who understand that everything is to be done to the glory of God. They directed their lives toward a purpose—and that simple difference has given them the impetus and energy to succeed where many others have failed.

In ancient days, all the craftsmen, artisans, and musicians proclaimed their godly purpose in life by what they produced. That's why the great classics of the world reflect a spiritual tribute to who God is. Through their endeavor, their work was beautiful and thus eternal.

In the twenty-first century few artists are creating works that will attain "classic" status. Why? Because most composers, sculptors, writers, and artists don't create their work to glorify God. Often what was once ugly is now considered beautiful, and what was beautiful has become ugly. Just look at our contemporary music, art, theater, cinema, and literature to see how we have strayed.

One of your duties as a mom is to watch and pray for your children. What are their talents? How can you help them discover their purpose? How can you encourage them to use their God-given gifts for His glory and not to merely follow the crowd?

God's desire is for you and for each member of your family to be purposeful human beings. To work toward meaningful goals and experience the joy of achievement.

So learn to live your life on purpose, and teach your children to do the same. If necessary, write out some obtainable goals and work toward them. Read books that motivate you toward your goal or that help you set worthy goals.

Above all, pray for God's guidance in your "on-purpose" life.

Prayer

Father God, give me purposeful direction on living a life that will glorify You. I'm tired of "shooting from the hip"; I'm weary of coasting. Help me choose wisely and move toward the right goals. Amen.

Action

Begin to live life on purpose. *What do you want to do to glorify God?*

∽∽∽∽∽∽∽∽∽∽∽∽

The greater danger for most of us is not that our aim is too high and we miss, but that it is too low and we reach it.

—MICHELANGELO

∽∽∽∽∽∽∽∽∽∽∽∽

Have the Courage of Conscience

...and be subject to one another in the fear of Christ.
—EPHESIANS 5:21

Last, but by no means least, [we must have] courage—
moral courage, the courage of one's convictions, the
courage to see things through. The world is in a constant conspiracy against the brave. It's the age-old
struggle—the roar of the crowd on one side and the
voice of your conscience on the other.
—DOUGLAS MACARTHUR

*T*he key thought for understanding Paul's view of proper
personal relationships in a Christian household is that the
subjection of spouses is to be *mutual* and based on reverence for God. For a couple, even a Christian couple, to
exhibit this attitude of humility in our secular world takes
great courage. The world doesn't understand the concept of
mutual submission to a mate. Instead, the media yell out,
"Submit to no one. Be *yourself*. Do what makes *you* happy."

But what does such a selfish attitude tell your children?
Rest assured, even the smallest child understands the tension between Mom and Dad that results when one partner

is acting selfishly. Don't be surprised then, when that same child models the same selfishness he's seen in his parents. Your child is learning from you *daily* how moms and dads relate to each other.

In most non-Christian cultures a woman is a second-class citizen. Not worth the same as a man. Many societies encourage men to lord over their women as though they were possessions. Even in America our thinking about husband/wife relationships is often non-biblical. And that attitude is passed on from one generation to the next as sons learn by watching their fathers and daughters by observing their mothers.

However, the Apostle Paul says that husbands and wives are to be subject one to another. That means that God places equal value on both. Each of us is created equal in God's eyes. We both are created in the likeness of God. How then should a husband and wife view each other? With mutual respect, affirmation, and honor befitting partners in life.

Partners look out for each other. Partners put the other person first—ahead of their own needs. This requires courage and a servant's heart. It also requires standing firm when co-workers, relatives, or well-meaning friends speak against submission in marriage.

Be brave. Stand tall. Don't let the roar of the crowd defeat the voice of your conscience. Do what's right in God's eyes. Your children will thank you for it.

Prayer

Father God, as my husband and I come together, give us courage to be subject one to another and serve one another. May our children see in us the heart of a servant toward our mate. Amen.

Action

As an exercise in humility, ask your husband what you can do for him today.

Today Is a Gift

We were burdened excessively, beyond our strength,
so that we despaired even of life.

—2 CORINTHIANS 1:8

*D*oes that Scripture sound like your life? Well, maybe not quite "despairing of life," I hope. But your complex role as a busy mom is almost beyond description. Without a doubt you have one of the most difficult, demanding, and taxing job descriptions in the world.

When I'm out and about shopping, I see you moms with your children, and I quickly think back to the day when Bob and I had five children in our home. I remember how tired I was—always! I never seemed to get enough rest.

Today the ever-increasing pressures and stresses of living are even faster paced, making it almost impossible for us to live the abundant life we all seek. Dad is pressured on the job. Profit margins are getting smaller, and competition is getting more fierce. While striving for excellence at work, Dad must also be a loving husband, father, and leader of his family.

Meanwhile, you as Mom have your stresses regarding the management of your household—keeping the children focused, satisfying your husband, and maintaining a proper balance in your life. What a recipe for stress!

But as Christians we can endure these stresses successfully if we view life's pressures as opportunities for us to demonstrate God's power. The following poem, which appeared in an old publication, *Record of Faith,* makes that point:

Pressed out of measure and pressed to all length;
Pressed so intensely, it seems beyond strength;
Pressed in the body, and pressed in the soul;
Pressed in the mind till the dark surges roll.
Pressured by foes, and pressure from friends,
Pressed into knowing no helper but God;
Pressed into loving the staff and the rod;
Pressed into living a life in the Lord;
Pressed into living a Christ-life outpoured.
—AUTHOR UNKNOWN

How we respond to our various pressures helps shape us into the person we will be tomorrow. If it takes all these stresses to make us into the person God has designed us to be, then all these uncomfortable situations will have made it all worthwhile.

Consider that your job as a mom is also God's means for revealing His strength as you tackle the duties you face daily.

Yesterday is history,
tomorrow is a mystery,
today is God's gift,
that's why we call it the present.

Look upon today as a gift. No matter what pressures the day brings—it truly is a gift for you. With each inconvenience you meet, may you realize that this too is merely a building block for whom God wants you to become.

Prayer

Father God, no one enjoys the pressures of life, but if I look at them as teaching tools for whom I am becoming, then I say, "Bring it on." Amen.

Action

Let today's pressure and stress teach you to live in the power of Christ.

The Lord's Prayer Speaks to Me

Our Father which art in heaven...
—Matthew 6:9

The unknown author who penned the following commentary on Jesus' model prayer challenges me as a mother when I recite the greatest prayer ever spoken.

I cannot say OUR if my religion has no room for others and their needs.

I cannot say FATHER if I do not demonstrate this relationship in my daily living.

I cannot say WHO ART IN HEAVEN if all my interests and pursuits are earthly things.

I cannot say HALLOWED BE THY NAME if I, called by His name, am not holy.

I cannot say THY KINGDOM COME if I am unwilling to give up my own sovereignty and accept the righteous reign of God.

I cannot say THY WILL BE DONE if I am unwilling or resentful of having it in my life.

I cannot say ON EARTH AS IT IS IN HEAVEN unless I am truly ready to give myself to His service here and now.

I cannot say GIVE US THIS DAY OUR DAILY BREAD without expending honest effort for it or by ignoring the genuine needs of my fellow men.

I cannot say FORGIVE US OUR TRESPASSES AS WE
FORGIVE THOSE WHO TRESPASS AGAINST US
if I continue to harbor a grudge against anyone.

I cannot say DELIVER US FROM EVIL if I am not prepared to fight in the spiritual realm with the weapon
of prayer.

I cannot say THINE IS THE KINGDOM if I do not give
the King the disciplined obedience of a loyal subject.

I cannot say THINE IS THE POWER if I fear what my
neighbors and friends may say or do.

I cannot say THINE IS THE GLORY if I am seeking
my own glory first.

I cannot say FOREVER if I am too anxious about each
day's affairs.

I cannot even say AMEN unless I honestly say, "Come
what may, this is my prayer."

—AUTHOR UNKNOWN

Prayer

Father God, thank You for teaching us how to pray. I
love to read and meditate on these powerful words.
They are so mighty. May my daily prayers be pat-
terned after Your 68 words of example. Help me to
live this prayer daily before my children who are
looking to me for wisdom. Amen.

Action

Pray the Lord's Prayer

Our Father which art in heaven,
  Hallowed be thy name.
Thy kingdom come. Thy will be done in earth,
  as it is in heaven.
Give us this day our daily bread.
And forgive us our debts, as we forgive our debtors.
And lead us not into temptation,
  but deliver us from evil:
For thine is the kingdom, and the power,
  and the glory, for ever. Amen.

—MATTHEW 6:9-13 (KJV)

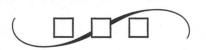

Not Too Much Spice

Then the Lord said to Moses,
"Take the following fine spices...."
—Exodus 30:22-23 (NIV)

It has been my privilege to author several cookbooks. As you might guess, my favorite room in the house is my kitchen. My love of cooking is perhaps inherited from my father who was a first-class chef for many prominent resorts and restaurants in southern California.

As a young child I would sit up on the kitchen countertop and watch Dad prepare gourmet meals for our family. Dad was such a perfectionist. Everything had to be just right. I can remember hearing him say, "Don't put too much spice in the food. You want to taste the flavor but not the spice."

I always remember that warning when I'm cooking.

Many times in my cookbooks I will put (optional) after some spices. Too much spice can spoil an otherwise excellent meal. Spices are to be balanced; they're not to overpower the natural taste of the dish to which they've been added.

So too in life. Spices are to be indulged *sparingly.* They are not the basic ingredients of life. Far too many of us try to live life with too much spice. We are bombarded with fun, pleasures, sex, erotic novels, long vacations, big cars, second and third homes.

After a while this spicy living makes us bored, and we seek out more and stronger spices. But when spices are used sparingly, they can enrich not only our food, but our life. As Dad used to warn, "Don't put too much spice in the food."

This is a great object lesson for children, as well as adults. Teach your children about the benefits of a life of moderation and illustrate to them the foolishness of a life with too much spice.

Prayer

Father God, I need balance when I cook. I don't want to ruin my entrée with spices that are too many and too strong. Let the spices enrich my food—and my life. Help me live a balanced, properly spiced life.

Action

Prepare a dish that normally calls for moderate spice. Allow your children to taste the dish seasoned properly. Then take a small portion and add more spice than is called for. Then let your child have a taste of this overspiced dish. Let them suggest ways that this can be applied to life.

Four Marriage Health Builders

And now abide faith, hope, love, these three;
but the greatest of these is love.

—1 CORINTHIANS 13:13 (NKJV)

*O*ne of the tragedies of divorce is that it prevents children from observing the proper model for a healthy Christian marriage. In my case, my model of what marriage is supposed to look like came from the very dysfunctional marriage of my parents. My dad had a drinking and temper problem. We never knew which Dad would come home—the out-of-control tyrant or the nice, loving father. I knew at a very early age that I didn't want a marriage like my parents'.

On the other hand, my husband, Bob, came from a wonderful family where the mother and father loved and cared for each other. His close-knit family was one reason I was so attracted to Bob. His was the kind of family I wanted.

We all enter marriage with some idea of what a marriage is meant to be, usually based on what we observed from our own parents, church, friends, and the prevailing culture in which we're raised.

But far too seldom do we take our pattern for marriage from God—the very One who designed marriage and family life to begin with. In the Bible, God offers some very basic principles for both husbands and wives.

One of these principles is given in today's Scripture, which lists three of the four virtues that give us a basic model for healthy marriage relationships: faith, hope, love. The fourth virtue, I believe, is justice.

David Augsburger, in his book, *Sustaining Love*, expands on these virtues. He says:

> Faith is the commitment to creative fidelity; it is faithfulness to each other before God. Faith is both a way of perceiving and of acting; it is believing and doing.
>
> Hope is the call of creative trust; it is hopefulness with each other before God. Hope is both a push from within the "hopeful" hoper and the pull from the possibilities of the future.
>
> Love is the choice to see the other partner as equally precious; it is lovingkindness that acts in equal regard. Love is a way of seeing, feeling, thinking, and acting toward another.
>
> Justice is the commitment to work out mutually satisfactory and visibly equitable sharing of opportunities, resources, and responsibilities in living with others; it is a creative drive for fairness in all covenantal relationships. Justice goes beyond retribution for injuries, and redistribution of resources to a redemptive and releasing discovery of what is truly right, good, and beautiful.[3]

Prayer

Father God, I'm grateful for how You give Your people a vision for a godly marriage. I always want to be a learner and to continue to grow in my walk with You. Please help me as I work toward making my marriage all You envision it to be. Amen.

Action

Tell your spouse how much you love him. Tell him one of the many things that you like about him.

~~~~~~~~~~~~~

Love Is...

Since long ago, people have searched for the meaning of love. But even the great philosophers, with their profound definitions, could not fully touch its true essence. In this survey of four-to-eight-year-olds kids share their views on love. But what do little kids know about love? Read on and realize that in their young and innocent minds, kids already have a simple but deep grasp of that four-letter word:

* Love is when you tell a guy you like his shirt and then he wears it every day.
* Love comes from people's hearts, but God made hearts.
* Love is that first feeling you feel before all the bad stuff gets in the way.
* When my grandmother got arthritis, she couldn't bend over and paint her toenails anymore. So my grandfather does it for her all the time, even when his hands got arthritis too. That's love.
* If life is "A," love is the whole alphabet.
* God could have said magic words to make the nails fall off the cross, but He didn't. That's love.
* Love is when a girl puts on perfume and a boy puts on shaving cologne and they go out and smell each other.
* Love is when you go out to eat and give somebody most of your french fries without making them give you any of theirs.
* Love is what makes you smile when you're tired.
* Love is when my mommy makes coffee for my daddy and she takes a sip before giving it to him, to make sure the taste is okay.
* Love is when you kiss all the time. Then when you get tired of kissing, you still want to be together and you talk more. My mommy and daddy are like that. They look gross when they kiss, but they look happy and sometimes they dance in the kitchen while kissing.
* Love is what's in the room with you at Christmas if you stop opening presents for a minute and look around.
* If you want to learn to love better, you should start with a friend who hates you.
* There are two kinds of love. Our love. God's love. But God makes both kinds of them.

—AUTHOR UNKNOWN

~~~~~~~~~~~~~

You Are Known by the King

*I am the good shepherd, and I know My own
and My own know me.*

—JOHN 10:14

*H*ave you ever had that sad, rejected feeling when someone didn't notice you? Your self-esteem sank low and you felt of little worth. You were lost in the crowd. You may have thought, *Who cares about little old me?*

In the midst of this computer age, it seems like we have become just an impersonal number—in fact many people are identified by just a number. When you call about a loan or a business-related item, the clerk will always ask, "What is your account number?" Even our junk mail is addressed impersonally to "resident."

As much as you might feel the sting of rejection, consider how much more intensely a child can feel rejected. Perhaps you remember the pain of being the last one chosen for a sports team, or watching your friends be asked to the senior dance by the most popular guys in class, while you sat quietly by.

When Edward VII, the king of England from 1901–1910, was visiting a city to lay the cornerstone for a new hospital, thousands of schoolchildren were present to sing for him. Following the ceremony, the king walked past the excited youngsters. After he was gone, a teacher saw one of her students crying. She asked her, "Why are you crying? Did you not see the king?" "Yes," the young girl replied, "but the king did not see me."

Those words of a child ring true to us as adults. We want to be noticed by those who are important to us. So too do our children crave attention—especially that of Mom and Dad. Make it a practice to *notice* your children. When they tug at your skirt with a question, don't ignore them. Give them the attention they crave. Also teach them early that there is One who is always there for them, even when others may reject them. His name is Jesus and He is always available to those who come to Him, especially children.

There was no way that King Edward should have been expected to notice every individual in that throng of people. Jesus, however, *does* give personal attention to every one who approaches Him. He calls His own sheep *by name*.

How does He do that? I'm not sure, but from experience I know He cares for me. I can hear His voice in Scripture and in song. How awesome to think that Jesus knows who I am. Perhaps this thought is even more awesome to our children. How can we or they have a poor image of ourselves when we are known by God? We are vitally important to the Creator of the universe. Amazing!

Prayer
Father God, thank You for making me more than my social security number. Thanks for knowing me. Help my children know too that they are known and loved by You. Amen.

Action
Tell the story of King Edward and the child in the crowd to your own children. Dramatize it and let them feel the sorrow of the child who wasn't seen by the king. And then tell them about another King who *does* notice all the children in the crowd.

All Your Days Are Ordained

My frame was not hidden from You,
When I was made in secret,
And skillfully wrought in the depths of the earth;
Your eyes have seen my unformed substance;
And in Your book were all written
The days that were ordained for me,
When as yet there was not one of them.

—PSALM 139:15-16 EMPHASIS ADDED

I am so thankful that one day my mother stood up to my father and said she would have no more abortions. She already had two previous ones to please him. Because of her bravery I was able to be born and to fulfill the life that God had for me.

Little did I know when I was conceived in my Jewish mother's womb that many years later I would accept Jesus as my Messiah and my personal Savior. My family did not realize that my name was long ago written in His book.

Life is so precious! We need to give every child in a mother's womb the opportunity to grow into the person that God has planned for him or her to become from the beginning of time.

31

Reach high, for stars lie hidden in your soul. Dream deep, for every dream precedes the goal.

—Pamela Vaull Starr

Prayer

Father God, life is so precious. I am forever thankful that You have ordained that I should have life. As a mother, may I be ever mindful of the preciousness of the life You create in the womb. Amen.

Action

Write or call your mother and thank her for giving birth to you. Consider making a contribution to a local crisis pregnancy center.

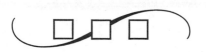

Ten Good Friends

A cord of three strands is not quickly torn apart.

—ECCLESIASTES 4:12

"I wish that I had some good friends to help me on in life!" cried lazy Dennis.

"Good friends! Why, you have ten!" replied his master.

"I'm sure I haven't half so many," sighed Dennis. "And those I have are too poor to help me."

"Count your fingers, my boy," said his master.

Dennis looked down at his strong hands.

"Count thumbs and all," added the master.

"I have—there are ten," said the lad.

"Then never say you have not ten good friends to help you on in life. Try what those true friends can do, before you go to grumbling and fretting because you do not get help from others."

—AUTHOR UNKNOWN

*M*any times we look to others to help us out, and we complain when we don't receive the help we think we deserve. However, help starts from within ourselves *first*, then comes from outside.

I know, as a busy mom, I often had to depend upon myself to get something done. Often there was no one around to help during the hectic schedule of a busy day. Perhaps your life is like that too. If so, take heart—you will get everything done that needs to be done.

At such times, it helps to take an inventory of all the skills and tools God has so graciously given us at birth. We tend to take for granted these attributes for success that were given to us at the very beginning of our lives—our eight fingers and two thumbs.

And although we need to dig in and do our own work, sometimes we *do* need the help of others. King Solomon in all his wisdom tells us that friends are great blessings to us. He says in Ecclesiastes 4:

> Two are better than one because they have a good return for their labor.
> ...But woe to the one who falls when there is not another to lift him up.
> ...if two lie down together they keep warm....
> ...if one can overpower him who is alone, two can resist him.
> A cord of three strands is not quickly torn apart.

Are you working on relationships that build these friendly blessings?

Begin at home with your family members. Throughout Scripture we are reminded to be united, be of the same spirit, be of one accord. Unity should be our goal: wife to husband, parents to children, children to siblings, friend to friend. Your church should be a source of help too. How well do you know the other mothers in your church? Have you reached out to offer help to another mother when she needs it? A good family church is a great place from which to build a network of moms who can help each other through the rough times of motherhood.

Prayer

Father God, let me fully realize the gift of my ten fingers that You have given me. May I also be appreciative of the other friends You have given me. Help me to be available to serve other mothers as I wish to be helped. Amen.

Action

Thank God for all the work your ten fingers do for you each day.

Search for Me

You will seek Me and find Me
when you search for Me with all your heart.

—Jeremiah 29:13

In ancient Greece a young man once approached the philosopher Socrates. The young man asked a simple, straightforward question. "Sir, how can I find truth?" Socrates invited the seeker to follow him.

As the story goes, Socrates waded into the Aegean Sea up to his waist. He commanded the young man to put his hands over his head. Socrates then placed his own hands above the boy's head. This was it—the moment of truth.

Socrates then pushed the lad's head under water. The young man struggled in Socrates' hands, fighting to come up for breath. The philosopher released his grip for a moment to allow the student a brief breath of fresh air. Then he quickly forced his head under water again.

Gasping for air, fearing he was going to drown, the young man came up for another breath shouting, "All I wanted was to find truth." The philosopher then zeroed in to the point. "Young man, when you want truth as much as you wanted that breath of air, you will find it."

Wow, what a level of passion it takes to want to know truth that desperately.

We are called to be seekers with all our hearts. When we seek for truth with that much vigor, God says we will find it.

It has taken a lifetime for me to know the measured amount of truth that I know. It hasn't come easy. I take three steps forward and two back, but at least I'm making progress. If you're discouraged by the "three steps forward, two steps backward" progression of your search for truth, be encouraged—at least you're headed in the right direction and God is with you all the way.

The fact is, few people could handle a speedier pace of maturity. Grow with God and don't worry about speed. Redwood trees take a very long time to grow—but their magnificence testifies to the worth of the wait.

The chances are, your children will only be as passionate about seeking the truth as you are. As Mom, you have a wonderful opportunity to model the life of a passionate truth-seeker before your children. Don't wait until they're older. Start teaching them about the importance of finding truth throughout life. Remind them of the One who said, "I am the way, the truth, and the life."

Prayer

Father God, I pray that I will have the passion to continually seek for truth. We live in a world that settles very easily for what looks like truth but isn't. Let me continue on until I find Your truth. Help me to model the life of a truth-seeker to my children. Create in them a passion for the truth—for *You.* Amen.

Action

Continue to seek for truth. Refuse to accept anything less. Tonight tell the story of Socrates and the truth-seeker to your children. Ask them if they understand the point of the story. Encourage them to be passionate about seeking the truth.

United We Stand

For this reason a man shall leave his father and his mother,
and be joined to his wife; and they shall become one flesh.

—GENESIS 2:24

*I*n union there is power. A single drop of water by itself is meaningless. But many single drops united by the force of attraction will form a stream, and many streams combined will form a river, until the rivers pour their water into the mighty oceans whose waves defy the power of man.

When forces act independently, they are utterly without power, but when acting collectively they have mighty strength. So it is with a husband and wife—particularly in their parental roles. When a mom or a dad operates alone, there is limited power in the family unit. But a man and a woman combined, each fulfilling their place in the family, makes for incredible strength and security—indispensable in raising healthy children. Disunity between Mom and Dad can result in insecurity and anxiety in children. Don't leave such a legacy to your children.

If we don't stand together as husband and wife, Dad and Mom, letting God make us one in spite of our differences, we will easily be defeated and so will our children. That's one reason why God calls a couple to

> Departure (a man will leave his father and mother)
> Permanence (cleave, or be joined, to his wife)
> Oneness (they shall become one flesh)

Becoming one doesn't mean becoming the same. However, oneness means sharing the same degree of commitment to the Lord, to the marriage, and to the children. Such oneness results when two individuals reflect the same Christ within. Such spiritual unity produces tremendous strength in a marriage and in a family.

For this togetherness to happen, the two marriage partners must leave their families (Mom and Dad) and let God make them one. As women, we help the cleaving process when we show our husbands that they are our most important priority after God.

If you clearly communicate your love to your husband, your marriage relationship will become more dynamic and your children will benefit.

Prayer

Father God, help me bring unity to our family. I want the peace that comes from harmony between a man and wife. I want our children to benefit from the gifts that a united mother and father can bring to the family. Help me in pursuing this goal. Amen.

Action

Are you a divider or a uniter in your marriage? Be willing to change into a person who unites.

~~~~~~~~~~~~~~~

How to Have
a Good Night's Sleep

1. Don't go to bed too hungry or too full. If you must eat
    before bedtime, limit yourself to a small snack.
2. Limit drinking all liquids a few hours before bedtime.
    That way you will reduce the chance of having to wake
    up to go to the bathroom followed by fighting to go
    back to sleep.
3. Avoid alcohol. It disturbs sleep quality.
4. Cut back on caffeine. It's a powerful stimulant.
5. Stop smoking. Nicotine is an even stronger stimulant
    than caffeine.
6. Get up at the same time every morning. Regularity
    helps keep your biological clock in sync.
7. Exercise every day. Get a minimum of 30 minutes of
    strenuous exercise a day.
8. Set aside time to unwind. Read, listen to good music,
    exercise, or just wind down before you go to bed.
9. Make your bedroom more inviting for sleep. Reserve
    your bedroom for sleeping and intimacy—don't turn it
    into an office or TV room.
10. Invest in a good mattress and pillows. The added cost
    will be one of your best lifetime investments.
11. Resist the urge to nap. For most people napping makes
    it harder to sleep at night.
12. Buy a pill box marked with the days of the week so you
    can check at a glance whether you took your medicine.[4]

~~~~~~~~~~~~~~~

The Grass Isn't Always Greener

If you keep My commandments, you will abide in My love....
—JOHN 15:10

Have you ever visited someone's lovely home and wished that it were yours? Or seen a new car going by and uttered, "Oh, that's what I want," or seen a hunk of a man and wished he was your husband?

It seems like we humans always want what we don't have. The grass always looks greener on the other side of the fence. Our pastor used to say the grass may be greener but it still has to be mowed.

There is a story of an old, but not wise, man. He sacked up his burdens and headed for the market to exchange them with someone who carried a lighter load. At the exchange booth, he met a man with a sack of gold. Now, no matter how heavy—that burden was worth bearing, the old man thought. But soon after the exchange he grew weary. The cumbersome, weighty bag of gold was worse than his previous burdens! So back he went, this time choosing a bag of silver. But the silver proved too heavy also. He mumbled and he grumbled all the way back to the exchange booth. This time he picked the lightest bag of all which to his delight contained sweet-smelling roses. How, he reasoned, could anything so lovely and lightweight be burdensome?

For the third time he started up the hill toward home.

But soon, ouch! The pricks of rose thorns jabbed him mercilessly with every bounce of the bag as he walked. With a sigh, he once again turned back and traveled down the hill, groaning in pain with every step.

By the time he arrived at the exchange booth, he had become a wise man—he exchanged the roses for his original sack of burdens and went away whistling merrily.

We often ignore the tenth commandment that warns us not to covet what another possesses. When we focus on the seeming blessings others have, we look away from our own many blessings.

Our children are by nature covetous. They see a friend's toy or bicycle and they want it for themselves. Or they notice how much better looking their friend is, or what a nice house he or she lives in, and they wish it were theirs.

Most children don't know what the word "covet" means. But when the meaning is explained to them, most will quickly understand—and see it in themselves. Teach them the virtue of contentment. It will be a great asset in the years ahead.

Prayer

Father God, clear my eyes from the green color of envy and jealousy. Let me see clearly the blessings You have given me. Help me teach my children to be content with all that You have provided. Amen.

Action

When envy comes in, go out with prayer. Count your own blessings. Tonight, share with your children the story of the unwise man who tried to exchange his burdens for someone else's. Make sure they understand how the story can apply to their life.

The Lone Ranger's Success Formula

Blessed are the poor in spirit,
for theirs is the kingdom of heaven.

—MATTHEW 5:3

When I was a girl, my brother and I loved to listen to the radio series, *The Lone Ranger*. Believe it or not I learned a lot of good life principles from that program. To this day, when I hear the William Tell Overture, my mind immediately flashes back to this great program that gave me my first exposure to good and evil.

What was this masked man's secret for success?

The Lone Ranger believed in

* Tolerance—The acceptance of other races through his close friendship with the Native American, Tonto.
* Fairness—Advocating the American tradition, which gives each person the right to choose a lifework and earn profit in proportion to individual effort.
* Patriotism—Love of country, which meant more than flag-waving and answering the call of war. It included aiding churches, serving the community, preserving law and order, and maintaining a proper home for bringing up the next generation of good citizens.

* Sympathy—Choosing the side of the oppressed in time of need. Demonstrating a strong man can be tender, the Lone Ranger is ever-forgiving.
* Religion—The right to worship God in individual ways. While the Lone Ranger was visualized as a Protestant, his confidants were the Native American Tonto and the Catholic Padre.

As moms we have the opportunity to teach life-lasting virtues to our children. Always be on the alert for times to talk about the importance of knowing the differences between good and evil. Even though we don't use silver bullets we can learn to use silver words.

Prayer

Father God, let my children look to my life as a standard for their lives. I pray they will see a mom who is always fighting against the evil and lifting up the good in life. Amen.

Action

Read the first eight beatitudes, Matthew 5:3-10.

As you read to your children, look for lessons to benefit yourself, as well. Most well-written children's stories have an underlying theme that we adults can often overlook. Listen to the story with the ears of a child.

Cleave and Become One

*A man shall leave his father and mother and
be joined to his wife, and the two shall become one flesh.*

—Matthew 19:5

*I*n today's social climate, it becomes more difficult for couples to join, or cleave, together and become one flesh. Bob and I have been married 46 years and at various seasons of life we have had to recommit ourselves to each other.

Our wedding was a lot of fun, but our marriage was much more difficult. We found that we had to stay flexible and not set anything in concrete (other than our faith in Jesus Christ). We had to learn to always keep open to one another, respect one another, and be willing to talk, talk, and talk.

On one of his broadcasts, radio host Bob Hammond shared the following poem entitled "On This Day":

> Mend a quarrel.
> Search out a forgotten friend.
> Dismiss a suspicion and replace it with trust.
> Write a letter to someone you miss.
> Encourage a person who has lost his faith.
> Keep a promise.
> Forget an old grudge.

Examine your demands on others and vow to
  reduce them.
Fight for a principle.
Express your gratitude.
Overcome an old fear.
Take a minute to appreciate the beauty of nature.
Tell others you love them and tell them again,
  again, and again.
And pray, pray, pray.

These are the actions that will speak loudest to your children. They're looking at you, Mom (and Dad), every day, for an example of how to live. Be united. Cleave together. Communicate with each other and respect each other. Give your children the best possible example of a Christian marriage.

Prayer

Father God, let me live this day as a strengthener of my marriage. Let me be willing to give myself to my mate. I pray that he will cleave to me and that we should become one. Help us to demonstrate our oneness to the children You have entrusted to us. Amen.

Action

Memorize Ephesians 5:21: *Submit to one another out of reverence for Christ.*

What to Do with Time Bandits

*...gather up the leftover fragments
so that nothing will be lost.*

—JOHN 6:12

Know the value of time; snatch, seize, and enjoy every moment of it. —LORD CHESTERFIELD

In the old McGuffey's Readers, the textbooks used by our ancestors, there's a story about a clock that had been running for a long time on the mantelpiece. One day the clock began to think about how many times during the year ahead it would have to tick. It counted up the seconds—31,536,000 in the year—and the old clock just got too tired and said, "I can't do it," and stopped right there. When somebody reminded the clock that it did not have to tick the 31,536,000 seconds all at one time, but rather one by one, it began to run again and everything was all right.[5]

As a busy mom, you never have enough time to get everything done, even without the interruptions caused by the various "time bandits" that rob us of precious minutes.

For instance, the doctor's appointment that runs late, the longer-than-expected grocery checkout line, the children's music lessons or sports activities that run longer than expected.

Time is easily lost on such days unless we learn how to make the best of these lost minutes. Here are some suggestions.

* Write a letter that's long overdue.
* Balance the checkbook.
* Plan your menu for the next week.
* Make out your grocery list to go with your menu.
* Read your Bible or a good book.
* Revise your "to-do" list, etc.

Prayer

Father God, don't let resentment set in when I have to wait, wait, wait. Let me take advantage of these "time bandits." Help me become a good steward of my time. Amen.

Action

Plan small projects during waiting periods. Most small chores can be accomplished in bits and pieces of time.

Consolidate phone calls, bill paying, and correspondence into a single time slot rather than responding to each one separately.

Time

Have you wished for wealth while dreaming
   of a goal
And thought that money was key to the plan?
Well, think again, for in any role
Time—not money—is the true currency of man.

Is it happiness you want, fulfillment of a dream,
Or will only power sate [satisfy] you, who fear to be
   an also-ran?
Well, reflect again on what success will mean.
It's time—not glory—that's true currency for man.

We are given one day to spend at each morn,
And what we do with this God-given gift
Will determine whether we are reborn
Or just waste away the sands that do sift.

So aim at the real treasures of man.
Think not about money or power or gain.
Rather, use the precious moments you can
And glory in Time, ere it slip by and wane.
—Richard B. Brown

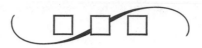

Naked and Not Ashamed

...the man and his wife were both naked
and were not ashamed.

—GENESIS 2:25

We live in a very sensuous era. We can't look at or listen to our media without being bombarded with erotic messages. We have to constantly be aware of what our children may accidentally see, lest they be exposed to explicit material. It's unfortunate that as Christians we have given the world control over what God created us to be—sexual human beings.

A healthy Christian marriage has the potential for greater depth than any other human relationship. How do we arrive at this trust level so we can stand before each other naked and unashamed?

Colleen and Lou Evans, Jr. shared in one of their books how this trust can be developed:

> And what is a friend? Many things....A friend is someone you are comfortable with, someone whose company you prefer. A friend is someone you can count on—not only for support, but for honesty.
>
> A friend is one who believes in you,...someone with whom you can share your dreams. In fact, a real

friend is a person you want to share all of life with—and the sharing doubles the fun.

When you are hurting and you can share the struggle with a friend, it eases the pain. A friend offers you safety and trust....Whatever you say will never be used against you. A friend will laugh with you, but not at you....A friend will pray with you...and for you.

My friend is one who hears my cry of pain, who senses my struggle, who shares my lows as well as my highs.[6]

Wow, what a tremendous relationship this kind of friendship exhibits within marriage. No wonder the couple can stand together naked and not be ashamed. This is the model of a godly love; this is the way it should be. However, don't hold your breath waiting to see this kind of love exemplified in our current culture. If your children are going to learn about the way a man and a woman are meant to love each other, it has to come from you and their father.

During their lifetime, your children will be barraged by the philosophy of love as seen by Hollywood. They will be told that sexuality is merely a means of gratification between two people. How will they respond? It's up to you. The groundwork for a right response must be put down *now.* Not only must you teach them the right place for sex, you must also guard diligently against the intrusion of wrong or immoral ideas about sexuality that may originate from your child's school, friends, television (including video), video games, books, and music.

If you do this job correctly, your future son- or daughter-in-law will thank you one day.

Prayer
Father God, show me how I can be a wife who will be pleasing to my husband. Help me teach my children

about the true meaning of sex between a husband and wife. Guard them against the images and philosophy of sexual immorality that are currently forming how our society views sex. Amen.

Action

Take the initial step to reach out to your husband as a friend.

Learn age-appropriate ways to share the facts of life with your children. Many fine books on the subject are available at your local Christian bookstore.

One Thousand Blessings

May the LORD, the God of your fathers,
increase you a thousand-fold more than you are and bless you,
just as He has promised you!

—DEUTERONOMY 1:11

To know that you will increase one thousand times and be blessed accordingly is almost beyond comprehension, isn't it? A CD (certificate of deposit) at the bank may pay six percent interest in good times, but a thousand percent markup is simply unbelievable.

Yet that's exactly what you're promised. In this verse, God says He will increase my blessings—and your blessings—a thousandfold. How can any beleaguered mom have a poor self-image or feel discouraged when our Father has promised us so much?

Of course this verse is talking about more than money. It's also talking about a return on your investment in family, emotional stability, marriage, health, desires, and all other components of life. And it doesn't have a time limit, either. Perhaps some of the blessings you're promised will happen in eternity and in the lives of those who come after you on this earth.

Either way, while on earth or in heaven, you must know that God keeps His promises—and what a promise this one is! This is a legacy for your children that far exceeds any earthly heirlooms you may leave them.

It really helps us to be thankful as we realize our blessings are growing and growing and growing—even amid the uncertainties of any adverse present situation.

Prayer

Father God, let me count my many blessings each day. As I look back over my life, You have already given me more than my thousand times increase. Amen.

Action

Take a journal and write down how God has increased you and is increasing you. Look under the microscope and see all the little increases as well as the big ones.

The Proper Posture
for Prayer

*Be anxious for nothing, but in everything by prayer
and supplication with thanksgiving
let your requests be made known to God.*

—PHILIPPIANS 4:6

*H*ave you ever thought, *What's the proper posture while I pray?* Or, *Is it all right if I pray while I'm standing at the sink, washing dishes?* Or, *What about when I'm doing my other motherly chores? If I pray then, will God hear me as well as when I'm on my knees in a quiet room?*

I've asked myself these questions, and in searching for the answers in the Word of God, I discovered that *all* positions are appropriate for prayer. God gives great liberty to praying people (especially praying *mothers!*). The important issue is that our hearts are in communion with God as we pray.

In the Scriptures we discover many ways of praying:
* Kneeling (1 Kings 8:54; Ezra 9:5; Daniel 6:10; Acts 20:36)
* Standing (Jeremiah 18:20)
* Sitting (2 Samuel 7:18)
* Lying prostrate (Ezekiel 11:13)
* In bed (Psalm 63:6)

* In private (Matthew 6:6; Mark 1:35)
* With others (Psalm 35:18)
* Anywhere (1 Timothy 2:8)
* Silently (1 Samuel 1:13)
* Loudly (Acts 16:25)
* For everything (Genesis 24:12-14; Philippians 4:6;
    1 Timothy 2:1-2)
* At all times (Luke 18:1)

Prayer is neither black magic nor is it a form of demand note. Prayer is a relationship. The act of praying is more analogous to clearing away the underbrush which shuts out a view than it is to begging in the street. There are many different kinds of prayer. Yet all prayer has one basic purpose. We pray not to get something, but to open up a two-way street between us and God, so that we and others may inwardly become something.

—JOHN HEUSS

Prayer

Father God, as I fulfill my calling as mother, please hear my every prayer—no matter what position I assume. Please know that I'm always kneeling in my heart. Amen.

Action

During the next week try several different physical positions as you pray. Read the Scripture given above that goes with each.

Harmony in the Home

...I pray that you, being rooted and established in love,
may have power, together with all the saints, to grasp how wide
and long and high and deep is the love of Christ,
and to know this love that surpasses knowledge—that you may
be filled to the measure of all the fullness of God.

—EPHESIANS 3:17-19 (NIV)

A traveler in Germany saw an unusual sight in the tavern where he stopped for dinner. After the meal, the landlord put a great dish of soup on the floor and gave a loud whistle. Into the room came a big dog, a large cat, an old raven, and a very large rat with a bell about its neck.

All four went to the dish and, without disturbing each other, ate together. After they had eaten, the dog, the cat, and the rat lay before the fire, while the raven hopped around the room. These animals had been well trained by the landlord. Not one of them tried to hurt any of the others.

The traveler's comment was, if a dog, a rat, a cat, and a bird can learn to live happily together, little children—even brothers and sisters—ought to be able to do the same.

Sadly, however, families are too often characterized by disharmony in the home. When that's the case, we do well to model our prayers for our family after Paul's words in today's Scripture reading. Such praying will surely lead to harmony in the home.

* Pray that your family may be "rooted and established in love" (v. 17). God's love can help us be patient and kind with one another. God's love is not rude, self-seeking, or easily angered.

* Pray that each member in your family would be able "to grasp how wide and long and high and deep is the love of Christ" (v. 18). Knowing that He loves us just the way we are, knowing that He made us special and unique, and knowing that He died for our sins enables us to love one another. When we grasp this, we can all love more freely.

* Pray that each family member would "know this love that surpasses knowledge" (v. 19). Because of our limitations, it's very difficult to fully comprehend God's love for us, a love that let Jesus die for us.

* Pray that each member of our family will be "filled to the measure of all the fullness of God" (v. 19).

What wonderful families we could have if each family member displayed these four basic qualities. Make Paul's prayer for the families of Ephesians your prayer.

Prayer

Father God, I pray that You would work in the hearts of our family to root and establish us in Your love. Amen.

Action

Pray this prayer for one week for you and your family.

Better to Give Than to Receive

For even the Son of Man did not come to be served, but to serve, and to give His life a ransom for many.

—MARK 10:45

One of the main purposes of the Christian life is to serve. The secular world usually wants to be served, but just as Jesus came to serve, so too are we to minister to those around us.

A few Thanksgivings ago our family decided that we were going to go with a group from our church to a downtown park and serve the homeless. The grandchildren who were old enough to help came along also.

It was so great to hear from those being served how good the food was and how appreciative they were for us giving up our Thanksgiving for them. Later, each one of our family members expressed that this was our very best Thanksgiving—spent doing what God wanted us to do, serving others. What a great way it was to demonstrate true thanksgiving to God for all His blessings.

The story is told of a man who rushed to the church door and asked if the service was over. The wise usher replied, "The worship is over, but *service* is only beginning." The service we render to others is really the rent we pay for our rooms here on earth. It is obvious that we are the travelers, and that the purpose of this world is not "to have and to hold," but "to give and to serve."

Ask any waitress and she'll tell you that her job is one of the best training fields for life. She's constantly busy for others and is daily exposed to all facets of life. Serving others has a way of keeping us humble in spirit!

Prayer

Father God, put a desire in my heart to serve others. My family is a great place to begin training. Let my attitude be one of service. Amen.

Action

Step out and serve! Try serving a shift or two in your local soup kitchen. Volunteer on a regular basis. If your children are old enough, be sure and include them.

Try putting an overnight guest in your child's room for the night and give your child the privilege of camping out in the living room. The result: an adventure for your child and welcome privacy for your guest.

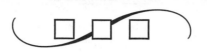

Take Time to Say "I Love You"

...Permit the children to come to Me; do not hinder them; for the kingdom of God belongs to such as these.

—MARK 10:14

In our "on-the-go" lifestyle, we don't often take the time to show love to our children. Time quickly passes by, and before you know it, they're soon too big to sit on your lap and too bashful to let you hug them.

Jesus knew that children were special and He often used them in His teachings. While you are blessed to have them in your home, take advantage of these years. If you don't, someday later you'll look back and say, "I didn't spend enough time with my children." But today you can begin to ensure that those words will never be necessary.

Don't let a day go by without saying, "I love you." Don't let a day pass without hugging your children. Speak kindly to them every day. Find something to laugh about with them. Explore with them. Play with them. Be a fun and loving mom.

The following poem by an unknown (but wise) author says it best:

> Dear little child: Today I told you you were too big
> to cry...too rough with the kitten...too careless with

crayons. I told you to share your toys, but I did not share my time. I was too busy to rock you and hum Brahms' "Lullaby"...

Dear middle-sized child: Today I reminded you your hair was too long...your hamster was hungry... and you were spending too much time with "that boy." I said drink your juice...match your sox...and study your spelling. But I had no time to help with the model airplane or look at your bug collection...

Dear teenager: Today I admonished you to keep your voice down and your shoulders up. Why was your bed unmade...your light on late...your phone call long? I said "No" to mascara...family car...and a school-night party. But I had no time to say you looked neat and that I was glad you made the team...

Dear child-gone-away: Today I sorted the possessions you left...and remembered you owe me a letter...promised pictures...and have not been home for—how long? But it did not occur to me to telephone you even though I enjoy your calls on my special days...

Prayer

Father God, let me take time to be with my children. Help me establish better priorities so I will take the necessary time. I don't want any regrets at the end of the day. Amen.

Action

Arrange a special time with each of your children. Be willing to *listen*.

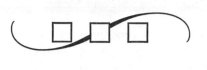

Who Am I?

But Moses said to God, "Who am I, that I should go to Pharaoh and bring the Israelites out of Egypt?"

—EXODUS 3:11 (NIV)

Have you ever asked a friend to tell you who they think you are? Even more challenging would be to ask your husband this question. Better yet would be to ask yourself.

If you're like most moms, you might come up with responses like these:

> I feel inferior to most of my friends.
>
> Sally is a better mother than I am.
>
> I don't like my hair.
>
> I'm too hard on the kids.
>
> I'm too easy on the kids.
>
> I don't have much real talent.
>
> My hips are too large.
>
> I need to lose 20 pounds.

You're not alone if you feel inferior. Most people do, to one degree or another. Even Moses struggled with feelings of inadequacy. He argued continually with God about his unworthiness to lead God's people out of Egypt. In Exodus 3:11, 13; 4:1, 10, Moses said, "Who am I?...What shall I say to them?...What if they will not believe me or listen to what

I say? I have never been eloquent…I am slow of speech and slow of tongue." Moses was full of resistance because of how he felt about himself and the calling on his life.

When we harbor negative feelings about ourselves and our role as moms, we stunt our growth as women of God. These destructive thoughts prevent us from reaching out to others, prevent us from responding to God, and inhibit us from becoming the women God wants us to become.

When God speaks to you, don't put up your hedge of resistance. He knows who you are and what you can do. He is calling you to be a mother to your children in spite of your pluses and minuses. He told Moses that He would be with him, that He would give him the right words to say, and that He would be Moses' mouth.

So too, as a mother you can depend on God to give you the grace and strength to be *exactly* the mother *your* children need. God doesn't make mistakes when He gives us the children we have. They're hand selected by God—and often they're the very means He wants to use to change us into the person we need to be.

When you're struggling with who you are, don't run away and hide, but talk to God about these feelings. Always remember that when God calls you to do something, He will always give you the strength to carry it out.

Prayer

Father God, thank You for making me in Your image. Give me the assurance that I can do all the mothering tasks I'm called to do, through the strength You provide. Amen.

Action

Talk to God about who you are. And even more— who He is.

Children Love Boundaries

A joyful heart makes a cheerful face,
but when the heart is sad, the spirit is broken.

—Proverbs 15:13

Men think God is destroying them because He is turning them. The violinist screws up the key till the tense cord sounds the concert-pitch; but, it is not to break it, but to use it tunefully, that he stretches the string upon the musical rack.

—Henry Ward Beecher

*P*arenting is an overwhelming task, and how to discipline our children is one of the most perplexing aspects in our job description. We often feel we are in a tug-of-war with our children. The natural tendency is to throw in the towel and give up (that's what the children hope for).

Far too often I've seen the sad results of parents who have given up their task of gently yet firmly shaping their children's will. The children grow up without boundaries, goals, or a purpose in life. Because they've not learned how to conduct themselves through the discipline that should have been administered by a loving parent, they now also lack the ability to discipline themselves.

But parents who take the time to shape their child's actions through discipline reap rewards both for themselves and their children. For all their complaining, children who battle the loving authority of their parents are actually greatly reassured when the response is consistent, firm, and confident. They find their greatest security in a structural environment where the rights of other people are protected by defined boundaries. One of the main purposes of discipline in our home was to have our children realize that they were responsible for their actions and accountable for their behavior.

One of the goals of parenting is to provide children with solid direction and self-assurance that will see them through life. I encourage you to read the book of Proverbs aloud to your children from an easy-to-understand version of the Bible. It contains some very good advice for both parents and children.

Prayer

Father God, grant me wisdom in disciplining our children. My husband and I want them to grow up as law-abiding and God-fearing adults.

Action

Evaluate your discipline process. What are you trying to accomplish?

Faith Is a Gift

Now faith is the assurance of things hoped for,
the conviction of things not seen.

—HEBREWS 11:1

My most cherished possession I wish I could leave
you is my faith in Jesus Christ, for with Him and
nothing else you can be happy, but without Him
and with all else you'll never be happy.

—PATRICK HENRY

$\mathscr{D}$o you ever have trouble believing in something you
haven't seen? The disciple Thomas did. He couldn't bring
himself to believe in Jesus' resurrection until he actually
saw and touched Jesus.

Jesus told Thomas, "Because you have seen me, you
have believed; blessed are those who have not seen and yet
have believed" (John 20:29 NIV). I don't believe Jesus was
scolding Thomas when He said these words. He was just
saying that Thomas would be a lot happier—that's what
"blessed" means!—if he could learn to take some things on
faith!

I think that's true for us moms too. Every day I take it on
faith that my car will start, my TV will click on, my Internet
Web site will function. I don't really understand any of

these things—they seem like miracles to me! But they work—at least most of the time!

So if I can manage to believe in these man-made miracles, why should I have trouble believing in God and His divine miracles? Though I haven't physically seen Him, I have felt His presence. I have seen His works. As a result, I no longer waste my energy fussing over whether God is real. Instead, I choose to enjoy the blessing of belief.

Prayer

Father God, I'm so thankful that I have not let the world system blind my eyes to You. You are there even with all the smoke screens of life. I know You are there even though I can't see You. Amen.

Action

Memorize 2 Timothy 3:16.

What Is Faith?

Faith is the eye by which we look to Jesus. A dim-
Sighted eye is still an eye; a weeping eye is still an eye.
Faith is the hand with which we lay hold of Jesus.
A trembling hand is still a hand. And he is a believer
Whose heart within him trembles when he touches the
Hem of the Saviour's garment, that he may be healed.
Faith is the tongue by which we taste how good the
Lord is. A feverish tongue is nevertheless a tongue.
And even then we may believe, when we are without
The smallest portion of comfort; for our faith is founded
Not upon feelings, but upon the promises of God.
Faith is the foot by which we go to Jesus. A lame foot
Is still a foot. He who comes slowly, nevertheless comes.
—GEORGE MUELLER

Never Stop Turning

You shall not add to the word which I am commanding you....
—DEUTERONOMY 4:2

ave you ever noticed how strong negative words are? Words like STOP, DON'T TOUCH, NO TRESPASSING, DANGER, DON'T ENTER, DON'T DISTURB OCCUPANT, BEWARE OF DOG, etc. The very words convey a commanding power.

When Scripture says "you shall not," we should heed this command. God doesn't issue meaningless warnings in His Word.

I can remember as a young girl the summer when Daddy had bought an old-fashioned ice-cream maker. The whole family was so excited when, one hot afternoon, he declared that he was going to make homemade ice cream. My mouth watered at the very idea, because our family had never made our very own ice cream. I was so excited!

As Dad was assembling the ice-cream maker, he was puzzled by the directions on top of the lid: "Stop turning handle when cream begins to freeze!"

These words were a little confusing, but being a man who followed directions, he complied. He stopped cranking when the wooden paddle became hard to turn, signaling to him that the cream had thickened. As instructed, he drained the salt brine from the bucket, covered it with an old blanket, and left it unattended so it could finish freezing.

We were so excited when mealtime came because we knew that dessert was next. We all gathered around Daddy as he very carefully lifted the lid from the container to make sure that no salt spilled over into the ice cream. We were all stunned when Daddy lifted the lid and there was luke-warm mix—nothing frozen. My brother and I broke into tears, we were so disappointed.

What happened? "If all else fails, read the directions," so Daddy reviewed the pamphlet. As he began to orally read its instructions, he came across these words, "NEVER stop turning handle when cream begins to freeze!" He had mis-read the instructions earlier, not seeing the crucial word "never."

As I look back over this disappointing experience, I can think about the importance of one negative word of warning—whether that word is "no," "not," or "never." When God utters these words, we are to pay special atten-tion. He means what He says.

Prayer

Father God, thanks for reminding me that *never* means *never*. I must continue to trust You when You use negative words to give me positive results. Amen.

Action

Believe God when He says NEVER. Teach your chil-dren the importance of being obedient to God's warnings. Show them, through Scripture, some of the consequences of those who disobeyed God.

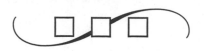

Being a Helpmate

...It is not good for the man to be alone;
I will make him a helper suitable for him.

—GENESIS 2:18

John Milton said it best when he wrote, "Loneliness was the first thing God's eyes named not good." God's creative act did not mean for man to remain alone. God made man to be gregarious and to be with others, and the first "other" was a woman.

Yes, you are to fulfill God's purpose for man not to be alone. You are to complement your man, and he's to complement you. Are you each succeeding in this role? Is he a better man because he married you? Do you complement your husband or do you compete with him?

As a partner in marriage, you are actually fulfilling God's purpose as you complete or give wholeness to your husband's life. Most men will never reach their full potential in God without a wife to help them reach for higher goals than they can set for themselves.

Dr. Dwight Small said it best:

> When a man and woman unite in marriage, humanity experiences a restoration to wholeness.... The glory of the man is the acknowledgment that woman was created for him; the glory of the woman is the acknowledgment that man is incomplete without her. The

humility of the woman is the acknowledgment that
she was made for man; the humility of the man is the
acknowledgment that he is incomplete without her.[7]

Many marriages are in ruin because of internal struggle
for power. But both partners must serve each other, not
ambitiously aim for a higher place than their spouse. Place
your ego at the foot of the cross and give it to Jesus. Become
a winner in marriage.

Prayer

Father God, let me share with my husband how my
life has been enriched by being married to him. He
means so very much to me. Amen.

Action

Tell your husband how much he means to you. Identify some specific ways he complements you.

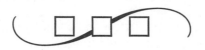

The Gift of Hospitality

...Be not forgetful to entertain strangers:
for thereby some have entertained angels unawares.

—HEBREWS 13:2 (KJV)

*O*nce a little girl wasn't able to see President Abraham Lincoln as planned. She had to stay home instead and was very disappointed at her lost opportunity. She was crying over her lot, when a knock came to the front door. A tall stranger was standing there in black. She courteously invited the man in for refreshments. After accepting a cup of hot tea, the man placed his hand on the child's head and smiled, "Tell your parents you entertained the president today!"

In olden days the mom of the house would put an extra potato into the pot just in case an unexpected guest dropped in at supper time. My Bob tells stories of how traveling men would walk along the railroad tracks in his hometown and often would drift off the tracks and wander into his neighborhood looking for food.

Bob's mom would always have leftovers to serve them. As far as we know, no angels were served, but Grandma Gertie was so happy to see how pleased these men were when they ate her delicious food.

Hospitality is a gift almost any mom can claim as her own. It may take practice, but learn to be giving with your food and your time. Teach your children to do the same.

Who knows, they may one day entertain an angel or a president.

Prayer

Father God, even though our culture is not as trusting as in older days, help me to be sensitive to those who come to me hungry. I can't feed the world, but I can help one at a time. Amen.

Action

Teach your children the meaning of the word "hospitality." Find a good way to demonstrate this word in action!

The Lord Is My Light

Do not rejoice over me, O my enemy.
Though I fall I will rise;
Though I dwell in darkness, the LORD is a light for me.
—MICAH 7:8

*T*he story is told of Satan's retirement party. The devil is going out of business, so he auctions off his most cunning deceptions. The evil angels bid higher and higher for each successive wicked strategy. The formulas for lust, lying, laziness, and many other sins are all auctioned off, each bringing a great price.

Finally after a long day of auctioneering, the devil prepares to close shop. He has one temptation left which he announces will not be auctioned off. The evil angels become furious. They press the devil into at least telling them what this final temptation is that he refuses to part with.

The devil responds: "The one temptation that I have left is the key to all the others. I use it especially on Christians. After you, my compatriots, use one of your temptations to get them to fall, I bring dark clouds of discouragement to sweep over them. Then I know I have them under my influence. This is the master stroke of deception with which I refuse to part."

Busy moms know all about this temptation. They can easily be discouraged as the clouds of darkness encroach. I experienced times when I was totally blinded by Satan. I thought I couldn't go on. I was tired, the children weren't behaving, money was short, bills had to be paid, groceries were too expensive, dirty dishes had to be washed, my husband was working long hours, and on and on and on. At such times, there didn't seem to be any light at the end of the tunnel.

But whenever Satan has a strategy, even a master strategy like discouragement, God has a remedy. The Scripture says that when we sit in darkness, the Lord will be a light to us. You mothers, when the world looks dark and you see no ray of hope, by faith look for God's light to penetrate your darkness.

When you find yourself down, get up and spring into action. Don't stay in your self-pity. Take on the day with new courage. Do not fear. You shall overcome. Keep looking for that ray of light from God your Redeemer. Offer Him praise and watch the cloud of discouragement vanish.

Prayer

Father God, there are times when life seems to spin out of control and I feel as though I have lost it. Then, O Lord, I look to You for your constant support and encouragement. Thank You for being there in my lowest moments. Thank You for Your light that shines in the darkest darkness. Amen.

Action

Claim God's promise that He will be there when you are discouraged. Get up; get going.

Teachable Moments

You shall teach them diligently to your sons and shall talk of them when you sit in your house and when you walk by the way and when you lie down and when you rise up.

—DEUTERONOMY 6:7

A certain philosopher was always talking to his friends about the gardens in which he was in the habit of walking and where he carried on his studies. At length one of them came to see him, and he found this extraordinary garden was a patch of ground about twice the size of the floor in his own bedroom.

"What!" said he. "Is this your garden? It's not very broad."

"No," said the philosopher, "it's not very broad; but it's a wonderful height!"

And so I would say to you parents. Your work at home is not a big place, but it's a wonderful height. It goes up to heaven.

Oh, what a profound idea: *your influence goes all the way to heaven.*

Don't ever forget that, Mom.

Sure there are other elements that have an influence on your children, but yours is the greatest.

You must be wise in how and when you teach. You have to be there to take advantage of those teachable moments that often come unannounced. They may come while driving, while on vacation, at night as you tuck your children in bed, at the breakfast table, or even after a church service.

No matter when or where, the writer of Deuteronomy instructs us to teach God's commandments:

> Sitting in your home
> Walking by the way
> When you lie down
> When you rise up

In essence, this training is like prayer—without ceasing.

Every moment is a time to teach. Don't let a single opportunity slip through your hand like sand on a beach. Be alert and sensitive to your children's need to talk. Look them in the eye and be transparent with their problems. Even though you may not feel their concerns are very important—*they* do. Be available.

Even today as a grandmother of five I take advantage of every teachable moment. I love it when my dear ones crawl on my lap and utter, "Grammy, what do you think?" They are so precious to me.

Your children and grandchildren will be much more stable and healthy in their Christian walk when over the years they have been able to talk about life's crucial issues from a biblical perspective with someone who loves them. You will have taken the time to teach whenever they have a need. This type of sowing will bring a full harvest. In fact your bushel will be overflowing with blessings.

Prayer

Father God, Your Son, Jesus, was an expert in taking advantage of those teachable moments. Wherever He was He was mingling with the sinners and He used those precious moments to teach. I want that same spirit of availability with my children. Amen.

Action

Today, watch for and take advantage of a "teachable moment." It will be there for you, *if* you're watching.

Enjoy the Whole Race

And let endurance have its perfect result,
so that you may be perfect and complete, lacking in nothing.

—JAMES 1:4

One day a hare was making fun of a tortoise for being so slow on his feet.

"Wait a bit," said the wise tortoise. "I'll run a race with you, and I'll wager that I win."

This idea greatly amused the hare and he agreed to the contest.

The race began and both the tortoise and the hare started off together, but the hare quickly took a commanding lead and was soon so far ahead he thought he might as well take a brief rest. So down he lay and fell fast asleep.

Meanwhile the tortoise kept plodding along and eventually reached the goal. At last the hare woke up with a start and dashed to the finish line, only to find that the tortoise had already won the race.

—AN AESOP FABLE

*D*o we see ourselves in this familiar story? Too many of us keep our eyes so closely on the start of the race, rather than its glorious finish. So much of life is painted with speed, flash, and sizzle that we can be intimidated if we choose a slower pace.

Several years ago Bob and I wanted to go to Los Angeles to see our son run in the famed Los Angeles Marathon. However, he discouraged us because he said we would see him for about a minute at the very beginning and five hours later we might see him finish.

A few years ago our family went to Lake Tahoe to ski during the Christmas holidays. As I walked on the icy slopes of this beautiful resort, my eyes saw the best the world has to offer—cars, ski clothes, and physical beauty. I had never seen so much sizzle in one place. So I thought to myself, *No way am I going to compete with this crowd.*

After being coaxed into my first ski lesson I found that members of that crowd I had judged as out of my league were also in my beginners' class, and they couldn't ski any better than I could. For all their fancy appearance, they were no better than I was.

Today's Scripture teaches that perseverance means enduring with patience. In the Bible, perseverance describes Christians who faithfully endure and remain steadfast in the face of opposition, attack, and discouragement. When we persevere with patience, we exhibit our ability to endure with calmness and without complaint.

Commitment, discipline, and perseverance are not words that the world is comfortable with. The twenty-first century will continue to be one where everyone wants everything to feel good—but perseverance doesn't always feel good. It sometimes demands self-denial and acceptance of pain.

Your children must learn this *from you.* If they enter the race unprepared, they will falter. Winning in life goes not to the fastest runner, but to the one who is guided by wisdom. And wisdom is the best gift you can give your children.

Prayer

Father God, in life's difficulties help me to look to You to see what You are trying to teach me. Let me slow down and not get ahead of Your program for my life. Amen.

Action

Take walks, explore the nearby woods, lake, or ocean-front, or even sit outside on the grass and appreciate the sights, sounds, and smells.

Slow down; pace yourself. Quit scurrying around like a squirrel preparing for winter. Life is a lot more fun when you're going slowly.

Someday Harmony

The wolf and the lamb will graze together,
and the lion will eat straw like the ox; and dust will be
the serpent's food. They will do no evil or harm....

—ISAIAH 65:25

What a great promise to think that some day in God's kingdom there will be perfect peace. That's when I want to have teenagers, don't you?

What would family life be like without the continuous fussing that goes on with sibling rivalry? No more pouting, loud outbursts, slamming doors, or borrowing unauthorized clothes from the enemy's closet.

Yes, what sweet peace that will be.

Once we owned a dog and cat who had figured out how to get along with each other. At night they would sleep cuddled up together on the same blanket. They had perfect harmony and were great friends. When our dog passed away, the cat was in mourning for some time—her friend was really missed.

What a state of peace when a wolf and a lamb can share their food together. When teenagers share clothes with great joy. When toddlers nibble from the same cookie jar without demanding the largest snickerdoodle.

Today's passage promises that one day we will experience this supernatural peace and harmony. In God's new world all His creatures will live in unity—what a wonderful day that will be. There will be no more fear—we will be secure in our surroundings. We can go out at night and not worry about becoming a crime victim—there will be no such thing.

Prayer

Father God, what a beautiful picture to imagine that someday we will all live together in perfect peace and be at harmony with all God's creation. In the meantime I will try to live that way in my present world. Help me establish a spirit of harmony in my home. May it be so real that the children take notice and act in peace toward one another. Amen.

Action

Jot down some ideas on how you can start to make your home a refuge—a place of peace and rest. Start by listing the things that presently detract from a peaceful home. Consider ways to change those distractions.

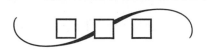

Grandmothers Are Wonderful

All discipline for the moment seems not to be joyful, but sorrowful; yet to those who have been trained by it, afterwards it yields the peaceful fruit of righteousness.

—HEBREWS 12:11

Grandmothers all over the world, we love you! You are

* The nurse who took over when Mommie worried about my fever, and bragged about my first tooth.

* The peppermint-scented lady who held me while she told Grandpa how to fix my broken toy.

* The capable hand holding mine during my first haircut; then, after calling tears "foolishness," stooped down to save a curl.

* The picture of courage walking me to nursery school, blowing my nose and powdering hers—never telling a soul we both cried like babies.

* The banker who insisted I give all my small allowance to Sunday school, then slipped dimes in my piggy bank so I could have the softball after all.

* The firm believer in "spare the rod and spoil the child" (with a switch "just in case").

* The "late reader" when I came back home from my first date.

* The schemer who helped me plan my wedding by taking over completely—all the while talking of the estimated 70 percent giving—on both sides.

* The not-too-subtle spokeswoman, telling me what a beautiful grandchild I was and that my parents deserved the same thrill.

* The memory whose teachings lead me to deal tenderly with my children, understandingly with my parents, lovingly with my husband, kindly with my friends, and obediently with God.[8]

Prayer

Father God, what a wonderful invention grandmothers are! Thank You for their influence and presence. Help me to appreciate my children's grandmother(s) even more. Amen.

Action

Write a note to your grandmothers (if they are still living) thanking them for all their care over the years. Have your children write a loving note to their grandmothers, expressing their love.

Giving Strength When Weak

He gives strength to the weary,
And to him who lacks might He increases power.

—ISAIAH 40:29

As a busy mom I was always tired. I yearned for more rest and sleep. The activities of the day often seemed beyond my strength. At no time in my life can I remember ever being so utterly drained of energy. Each day I looked forward to evening when I could tuck the children into bed and get some well-needed rest.

Looking back, I'm sure those days weren't much fun for my husband, Bob, either. When he came home from work, my energy had long since been sapped by the day's activities. By age 21, I was responsible for five children—our two and my brother's three children whom Bob and I took in. Life at that time absolutely overwhelmed me.

At such times of low physical reserves, we are open prey for the enemy. Satan can attack us with all sorts of accusations about our lot in life. His goal is to cause us to resent the demands made on us and to cast doubt on God's faithfulness.

But God knows our weaknesses and in every case will send the strength we need for every day's circumstances. No more, no less. Just enough.

Mom, don't be discouraged by your weaknesses. God knows your need. He really does. It's human to be tired after a mom's full day, but how we handle our tiredness is of utmost importance. Our power for living *must* depend on faith in the source of our power—Jesus Christ.

During times of extreme stress, look fully to His great promise that He gives power to the weak and He increases strength to those who have no might. Claim this as your "tired promise." Do it as often as necessary—*even if it's every day!*

Prayer

Father God, when I feel weak, let me rely on Your strength. I will not let Satan take advantage of my tiredness. Instead I turn to You and receive the victory set aside for me in Christ. Amen.

Action

Exchange your weakness for God's strength.

The Four "With Alls"

And you shall love the Lord your God with all your heart, and with all your soul, and with all your mind, and with all your strength.

—Mark 12:30

Since the 1960s our culture has followed the loose philosophy of "do your own thing." You know the mottoes: "I know what's best for me." "Don't tell me what to do." "If it feels good, do it." In the wake of this value shift, we've seen an increasing lack of accountability with each succeeding generation.

In contrast, one noted Christian said, "The rule that governs my life is this: Anything that dims my vision of Christ, my prayer life, or makes Christian work difficult, is wrong for me, and I must, as a Christian, turn away from it."

Which motto do you want your children to embrace as they grow up? Be assured, the former message will be broadcast loud and clear *repeatedly* throughout their life. If they're going to learn anything different—if they're going to grow up with godly values and a willingness to assume responsibility for their actions, it's up to *you* to instill that philosophy in them.

Search your heart today and see if you're setting an example as a mother who accepts her responsibilities readily, admits her mistakes with grace, and serves God's will with all her being.

How are you to love the Lord?

> With all your heart
> With all your soul
> With all your mind
> With all your strength

Prayer

Father God, give me the will and power to love You with these "with alls." I want to continue to have the passion to love You this way every day. Amen.

Action

Make choices that are guided by your love for God. Teach your children to do the same.

Be Angry at Evil

Be angry, and yet do not sin;
do not let the sun go down on your anger....

—EPHESIANS 4:26

*A*nger is one of the most difficult emotions to keep under control—especially for frazzled moms. It's normal to exhibit some form of anger at times. Anger itself isn't evil—God gets angry at times, and so do we.

God gave us the emotion of anger as a response to evil in the world, or, on a smaller scale, as a way of showing displeasure when our child has acted wrongly.

Though anger itself isn't wrong, how we express this anger determines if we have sinned or not. When we find ourselves angry at a person or situation, we need to try to find a way to fix the problem objectively, rather than just using anger as a vent to release negative emotion.

For instance, you might say, "I'm really hurt and angry over this situation and here is what could help solve this problem." This is making a positive statement rather than heaping fire on the situation.

My Bob and I have used today's Scripture verse many times in our marriage and with our children. We have often talked through and prayed through our differences of opinion. Many times Bob and I have talked late into the night in order to come to an agreement.

In contrast, we've seen other couples, other parents, whose wrong responses to anger have turned destructive to both their marriage and their children. What a price to pay!

What then must we do with our anger?

First, remember that most anger is caused by hurt, fear, or frustration. Identify the initial cause of anger and prayerfully look to Scripture for a solution. Some verses that deal with anger include Proverbs 14:29, Job 5:2, Proverbs 15:18, and James 1:19.

Second, make your anger a positive force. If your anger is directed at your mate, talk about ways you can help each other resolve your disputes without turning destructive.

If your children are a constant source of anger, it's a signal that some changes need to be made in your parenting techniques. *Never* allow your anger to overflow into physical actions toward your child. Discipline, especially, should never be administered in the heat of anger.

One good resource for moms is *She's Gonna Blow!* by Julie Barnhill. Other good books on the subject can also help. Unresolved anger can lead to health problems. This is an issue that you must make a priority. A constantly angry mother will produce frustrated, insecure, and unhappy children.

Prayer

Father God, let me study why I'm angry. Let me know myself better. I cast all my fears upon Your altar. Give me humility so I walk in the spirit of God and not filled with the flesh. Amen.

Action

Do not let the sun go down on your anger. Pray with whoever is causing you anger.

Knowing God

How long, O LORD, will I call for help, and You will not hear?
—HABAKKUK 1:2

All of us have reasons to ask, "Lord, why me?" from time to time. As we journey through life, we will have a lot of unanswered questions. But really, we don't need to know everything here on earth. Our mind is not always able to comprehend God's ways, for His ways are different from ours. That's why God calls us to trust Him in everything, especially when we ask, "Why me, why this?"

Through a recent serious illness I have echoed Habakkuk's plea, "How long, O Lord, will I call for help and You seem not to hear me, not only me but thousands of my prayer supporters, too?"

Through this time I've learned that waiting without an answer gives me an opportunity to learn to live by faith. Without a doubt my faith is bigger, better, and stronger today than when I first was diagnosed with cancer. I have been tested and my spiritual muscles are stronger.

Perhaps your "Why me, Lord?" question revolves around your children. Perhaps you have a child with a health problem or with a disposition that is contrary to yours. Our children are gifts of God and no matter what has happened to you as a mother, God is in control. You may or may not ever know the answer to "Why me, Lord?"

But you can learn to trust implicitly that there *is* an answer to that question in God's mind. And, if you trust in His wisdom securely, the day will come when you will no longer need to even ask the question—it eventually becomes irrelevant to the trusting lover of God.

Habakkuk, though he challenged God because of unanswered prayers, eventually came to the great verses of 3:17-19 and announced,

> Though the fig tree should not blossom
> And there be no fruit on the vines,
> Though the yield of the olive should fail
> And the fields produce no food,
> Though the flock should be cut off from the fold
> And there be no cattle in the stalls,
> Yet I will exult in the Lord,
> I will rejoice in the God of my salvation.
> The Lord God is my strength.

Yes, through all of our unanswered "whys" we can exalt God and know that He is our strength.

Prayer

Father God, You are my Lord and strength. In all that I experience I know that You are with me and that You will never leave me. I exalt You. Amen.

Action

Rejoice heartily in the God of your salvation.

Let Your Home Belong to God

*You shall write them on the doorposts
of your house and on your gates.*

—Deuteronomy 6:9

*S*hortly after Scottish preacher G. Campbell Morgan's wedding, his father visited the new home the newlyweds had just furnished and decorated. After they had shown him around the home with pride and satisfaction, the father remarked, "Yes, it's very nice, but no one walking through here would know whether you belong to God or the devil!"

Morgan was shocked by his father's gruff but well-meaning comment. But the son got good old dad's point. From that day forward, he made certain that in every room of his home there was some evidence of the new family's faith in Jesus.

In many of my books on hospitality, I share with the readers the idea of having a welcoming plaque in their front-porch area. This gives visitors an indication that they are welcome into your Christian home. It also reminds your children that they *live* in a Christian home—one that honors Christ. These silent witnesses will daily reinforce the idea that their home is a place where Christ is the head of the house.

You can also have other reminders around the house:

* Bible verses inscribed on plaques.
* Tasteful Christian art (there's so much more of this to choose from these days).
* Christian books and magazines on coffee tables and in reading areas.
* Whenever appropriate, worshipful selections of Christian music—instrumental and vocal—playing in the background.
* A blackboard near the front entrance where you can print a verse of Scripture, or jot a praise of some family member. You can also write a note to guests who are visiting. They'll love seeing their name on the blackboard announcing their welcome.
* If you have a banner pole, fly Christian-related banners celebrating special times of the year—Easter, Thanksgiving, Christmas, etc.

Change and rearrange these reminders often, keep the sentiments fresh, and draw attention to the Lord we serve.

Prayer

Father God, You are a "God of Remembrance." I love to tell my children, friends, guests, and neighbors how much You mean to me. These silent witnesses are a wonderful way to express to all that Your presence is very important in this house. Amen.

Action

Select one way you can signal to your guests that they are in a home that loves the Lord, then do it.

What Makes You Happy?

To everything there is a season,
A time for every purpose under heaven.

—ECCLESIASTES 3:1 (NKJV)

*O*nce upon a time there lived a family of happy owls. The barnyard animals, who were forever squabbling, demanded, "Why are you so happy?"

Mama owl replied, "When spring comes, we're happy to see everything come to life after the long winter sleep. The trees put forth their buds and leaves; the meadows are covered with thousands of tiny flowers; and birds everywhere are singing merrily. Later, around every flower, bees and bumblebees are buzzing, and all kinds of little flies are humming. Butterflies flit to and fro, gathering honey from the golden sunflowers. Then we know that summer is here....Then autumn comes, and the spider, who has waited through the glorious summer under leaves, comes out and spins her web to hold up the tired leaves a little longer. We rejoice to see her, and finally when the leaves are fallen and the earth is covered with snow, we come back and are cozy in our old home—for winter is here again."

The secret of happiness for this wise owl family is their ability to see and rejoice in the pattern of life as revealed through the four seasons God has given us.

If we take time to observe, nature is a great reminder of God's faithfulness to us, as everything happens in its season.

Like nature, motherhood has its seasons. Sometimes when our children are young and full of energy and "but why, Mommy" questions, we think the season will never change. But what we may see as the harsh winter of discontent eventually turns to other seasons as the children grow older.

Someday (sooner than you think!) the season of your motherhood will change into something entirely different from what you're experiencing now. The baby you nurse at your breast will become a bundle of energy zooming from here to there in a wink. And then the child will become a boisterous teenager, presenting a new season of motherhood challenges. And then, before your very eyes, your children will have become independent adults, leaving home.

You will always be their mother, but the season will change. The happiest mothers I know are those who learn, like the wise mama owl, to treasure each season as they pass through it.

If you wait and look back at the past seasons with longing and regret, you will turn what should be your summer of happy remembrances into yet another winter of discontent. Don't let that happen to you. Whatever season you're in, rejoice in it, anticipating the grand new seasons rapidly approaching, for each season brings its own special rewards.

Prayer

Father God, I thank You for the gift of my children. I thank You too for the season of motherhood through which I am currently passing. May I experience every joy You have for me during this season. Amen.

Action

Find happiness in all the day's events, for this is the season of your motherhood. Enjoy it.

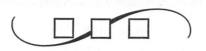

Be Your Husband's Mirror

*Now to Him who is able to do far more abundantly
beyond all that we ask or think, according to the power
that works within us...to Him be the glory....*

—EPHESIANS 3:20-21

Peter Foster was a Royal Air Force (RAF) pilot during World War II. RAF men were the cream of the crop of England's young manhood. They were the brightest, healthiest, most confident and dedicated (and often, the most handsome) men in England.

The scene in London, however, was far from romantic. The Germans were attacking relentlessly. For 57 consecutive nights they bombed the city. In waves of 250, some 1,500 bombers would approach each evening and pound the city with huge bombs.

The small airplanes that pilots such as Peter flew looked like mosquitoes pestering the huge German bombers. In addition, these English airplanes had a major design flaw. The single propeller was mounted in front, only a scant foot or so from the cockpit, and the fuel lines snaked alongside the cockpit toward the engine. On a direct hit from the enemy, the cockpit would erupt into an inferno of flames, and the pilot's body would literally burn away.

Any RAF pilot who happened to survive a hit would undergo a series of 20-40 surgeries to refashion what once were his face, hands, and arms. Plastic surgeons worked miracles, yet what remained were essentially scars.

Peter Foster was one of those surviving pilots. Each day in the hospital as he recuperated from surgery, he looked in the mirror—worried what his friends and family would think of his unrecognizable face. And with each look in the mirror, he dreaded the day when he would be sent home.

He had been told about other pilots who had returned home to terrible experiences. Many went through divorce, some chose suicide, and others became prisoners of their own homes. Some, however, returned home to accepting, loving families with very few transition problems. Peter hoped that would be his lot.

The day soon came when Peter's fiancée came to the hospital for a visit. As he looked in the mirror while awaiting her arrival, he worried that she would be repulsed by his new look and reject him.

But when she arrived, Peter's girlfriend easily accepted the same man she had known before his tragic disfigurement. She assured him that nothing had changed except a few millimeters of skin. She told him she loved *him*, not his facial membrane. The two were married before he left the hospital.

In reflecting back, Peter said, "She became my mirror. She gave me a new image of myself. Her warm facial expression told me I was okay—it still does, years later. She makes me alive and gives me great confidence."

We reflect to our mates and our children acceptance or rejection by our verbal and nonverbal communication. They derive much of their worth from how we relate to them. In order for our husbands to feel worthy they need a wife who will reflect acceptance. Our children too need that same message *repeatedly* communicated to them. This is especially true if we have a child who perceives him or herself to be physically unattractive.

Always remember that you are the mirror for your husband and your children. What you tell them that you see when you look at them is what they too will see.

Prayer

Father God, let me be my family's mirror. What a great responsibility! May I look for only beauty in each family member—and may I always remember to communicate to them the beauty that I see. Amen.

Action

Find wholesome words of praise today for each member of your family. Compose a short poem of praise for each of your children and lay it on their pillows where they will find it at bedtime.

Wait for the Unfolding of God's Plan

Rejoice always;
pray without ceasing;
in everything give thanks;
for this is God's will for you in Christ Jesus.

—1 Thessalonians 5:16-18

During the past few years, as I've battled a serious disease, I've witnessed a new depth and understanding of this thing called prayer. For the longest time, I couldn't understand how one prayed without ceasing. How could one do that? After all, we busy moms have other things to do each day besides pray.

But let me tell you, when you face a life-and-death crisis, and when every doctor's appointment reveals possibly how long you will be with your family and loved ones, you quickly learn to pray without ceasing. When your child faces a dangerous illness or is otherwise threatened, you'll know that praying without ceasing *is* possible.

But we don't need to wait for adversity to pray without ceasing. Nor should we assume that we will automatically know how to pray when that day comes. Sometimes our prayers need to include these words: "Lord, please give me the insight to know *what* I am to pray for and what You desire for my life. Give me the patience to wait for Your timing in answering my prayer. And give me the ability to handle answers which I did not anticipate."[9]

God does answer our prayers, but when the answers may not be what we expect, we would do well to heed Dr. Lloyd John Ogilvie's advice:

> Because God can see what we cannot see, and knows dimensions that we can never understand, He works out our answers according to a higher plan than we can conceive. We are to tell Him our needs and then leave them with Him. It's only in retrospect that we can see the narrowness of our vision and can see that His answer was far better than what we could even have anticipated.
>
> Prayer is not just the place and time we tell God what to do, but the experience in which He molds our lives. In the quiet of meditative prayer, we begin to see things from a different point of view and are given the power to wait for the unfolding of God's plan.[10]

Prayer

Father God, don't let me try to get ahead of Your timetable. I want to try to understand Your will for my life and for the lives of my children. Give me the power to wait for the unfolding of Your plan. Amen.

Action

Trust God for His plan for your life.

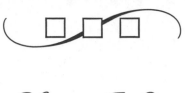

Live It Out

*In everything, therefore, treat people the same way you want
them to treat you, for this is the Law....*

—MATTHEW 7:12

*E*ven on secular talk shows you hear people agree that
practicing the Golden Rule is the best way to live. They
mostly agree that if we live out the Golden Rule and the
Ten Commandments we will find real happiness and joy
in our earthly walk.

But practicing the Golden Rule isn't part of our standard
equipment as human beings. Someone had to teach it to us
or demonstrate it. And when they did so to our benefit, we
were pleased, and we learned that this consideration of
others is a good thing to do. We learned it because we were
learning to do to others what we would like others to do to
us.

Often while grocery shopping, when I notice that the
next customer behind me only has two items, I will offer to
let that person go ahead of me if I have a full cart. I'm sure
this is something that I learned when very young. I may
have seen my mother or some kind stranger do it.

Another example is when you're pulling out of a parking
lot into a traffic jam. If some courteous driver didn't practice the Golden Rule, you'd sit for hours trying to ease your
way into the flow of traffic. But because I've seen others do

this often, I also do it. It's called kindness. Courtesy. Thinking of others. *The Golden Rule.*

If I asked your children, "What's the Golden Rule?" what would they answer? Do they know and practice this bit of ancient wisdom? Do they see you practice it at the supermarket or on the highway?

Live by the Golden Rule. It will make for a happier world not just for yourself, but for everyone you come in contact with.

Prayer

Father God, let my kindness be a reflection on who You are. May others see You by experiencing me as I live out the Golden Rule. Amen.

Action

Tonight at dinner, discuss the Golden Rule with your family. See if they can suggest ways it can be practiced at home—perhaps at the very dinner table where they're sitting.

Love Is Better Than Wine

May he kiss me with the kisses of his mouth!
For your love is better than wine.

—Song of Solomon 1:2

There are many who want me to tell them of secret ways of becoming perfect and I can only tell them that the sole secret is a hearty love of God, and the only way of attaining that love is by loving. You learn to speak by speaking, to study by studying, to run by running, to work by working; and just so you learn to love God and man by loving. Begin as a mere apprentice and the very power of love will lead you on to become a master of the art. —St. Francis de Sales

Francis de Sales might also have mentioned the art of mothering. How does one become a master at mothering? By simply beginning as an apprentice and moving up toward journeyman (journeywoman?). We learn to mother by jumping in with both feet and *doing it.*

Almost anything that we women are called to do is best achieved not by listening to long lectures by the "experts" or even reading books by well-known authorities. The best way is on-the-job training. Our mother-in-law and dear old mom will offer some very good advice—much of which we will want to implement. But sometimes you'll find a new and different way works best for you. Let your mothering style be *yours*, matched to the particular needs of your children and mate.

Even the experts had to learn firsthand what works best—and so do you. Remember too that every child is different. For instance, in the area of discipline, some children respond to corporeal punishment while others are chastened more by a temporary restriction of their favorite activity.

Relax, you'll find out what works best for you as a mother—with some experimentation.

Prayer

Father God, help me learn to be the unique mother my children need. Send the best advice my way, but help me learn to recognize it when I hear it. Give me discernment so that I can tell the wheat from the chaff. Amen.

Action

Start a notebook of special mothering advice *to* yourself, *from* yourself. Every so often add little snippets of wisdom unique to your mothering situation and style.

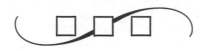

And They Went to Sleep

*Cast your burden upon the LORD
and He will sustain you....*

—PSALM 55:22

There was this man who owed his next-door neighbor a hundred dollars. The bill was due the next day, and the debtor only had 30 dollars. That night the man was so anxious about the next morning that his tossing and turning kept his wife awake. Finally, exasperated, she got out of bed, threw open the window, and yelled to the neighbor, "Hey, Ruben! About the hundred bucks—he ain't got it!" "Now," she said to her husband, "let him worry!" And they went to sleep.

Have you ever tossed and turned because you are worrying about some issue in life? Perhaps your child? Your husband? A job? A mistake you made?

This worry keeps replaying itself in your head. You fret, lose your train of thought, and become stressed out. All the while, if you'd remember today's psalm, you could relax and go to sleep. When God says to cast your burden upon Him and He will sustain you, He means every word of that promise.

I have prayed more in the past four years than I've ever prayed. During this walk with cancer, God and I have become very close. I've meekly prayed, I've prayed with anger, with tears, with a pitched voice, with petitions, with praise, and with thanksgiving. And God heard me each time and has sustained me.

He will sustain you too. Not only that, *He will work out the problem that's plaguing you, no matter what it is.* God delights in being our God. Don't rob Him of the joy He gets from shouldering your burden for you.

He truly wants to help.

Prayer

Father God, I don't want to be a martyr and rob You from helping me. I want to be more transparent with my daily problems. You know what they are. Thanks for being concerned about every one. Thanks for being here with me. Amen.

Action

Reveal to God what you need from Him—the big and the small.

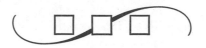

The Difference Between Two Roads

...lead me to the rock that is higher than I.

—Psalm 61:2

There is a story about two small roads that ran side by side. They chatted as they wound in and out of country places, laughing with the brook, sighing with the wind, and resting now and then along the level knolls. There they watched the trees put on their green gloves in springtime, raise their leafy umbrellas for summer shade, wind tawny shawls around their shoulders in autumn, and lace their limbs with snowflakes when winter came.

They were very happy little roads because they did their jobs well. Schoolchildren walked upon them, and wagons rolled smoothly upon them. Shy little creatures played games along their ruts when nobody was near. On and on they went until at last they came to a little incline. One road panted at the effort, but the other road encouraged it to come along. The hill eventually grew steeper, and the tired road said, "I can't make it. I'm going back." The other road worked very hard and grew very weary, but at last it came to the summit and danced over into the world beyond.

As we travel through life, most of what we encounter is pretty easy. But when we occasionally reach the steep hills, we come to a screeching halt. These hills seem to be barriers to our dreams and wishes about life. We're tempted to turn back because we become tired and can't make the steep climb to the top of the hill.

But the mother who faces such challenges, the woman who can discipline her life through the hardships and setbacks, will soon sail over the summit of the hill and down the other side into the glorious valley of victory.

Prayer

Father God, I want to be able to finish the race. Give me abundant endurance to follow You all the days of my life, particularly when the hills of motherhood become steep. Amen.

Action

Strengthen your walking muscles so that you can climb steep hills. A good, brisk, or even leisurely walk is a great break from a trying day.

God Knows My Name

...I have called you by name; you are Mine!
—Isaiah 43:1

*C*harles Haddon Spurgeon once said, "He who counts the stars, and calls them by their names, is in no danger of forgetting His own children. He knows you as thoroughly as if you were the only creature He ever made, or the only saint He ever loved."

One of the advantages of living in a town for a long time is that people know your name. No matter where you go— to the bank, to church, to school, to the pharmacy, or to the car wash—they all say, "Hello, Mrs. Barnes."

This tells me they care, they have an interest in me—and it also makes for good business. One of my brothers-in-law patronizes a certain restaurant because they greet him by name every time he enters. When he entertains a guest for a meal, he likes the guest to know that the restaurateur knows Mr. Barnes by name.

My Bob knows he's in real trouble when I address him with, "Barnes." He then begins to really pay attention.

God knows you by name. He summons you and you are His. How awesome this is to believe. You don't belong to anyone else. You are *His*. That's what makes us all so special; we are God's children. When you address your family members, remember that they too are owned by God—they are His children. Treat them with the respect due God's children.

Prayer

Father God, since I am Yours and You are mine, I want to respect You and Your position. Let my speech approach You accordingly. Amen.

Action

Be sure and learn the names of your children's friends. Address them by name when they come to play. Notice them. Most parents don't really pay much attention to their children's friends.

My Neighbor's Bible

I am my neighbor's Bible,
He reads me when we meet;
Today he reads me in my home,
Tomorrow in the street.
He may be relative or friend,
Or slight acquaintance be;
He may not even know my name,
Yet he is reading me.

—AUTHOR UNKNOWN

Making Your House a Home

Unless the LORD builds the house,
They labor in vain who build it;
Unless the LORD guards the city,
The watchman keeps awake in vain.

—PSALM 127:1

$\mathcal{A}$s busy moms, we sometimes wonder if we actually have a home—or is it merely a stopover place to eat, do laundry, hang around, and sleep? Or is it just a place to repair things, mow the law, paint, wallpaper, and install new carpet? A true home is much more than all that. It's a place of people living together, growing, laughing, crying, learning, and creating together.

A small child, after watching his house burn down, was quoted as saying, "We still have a home. We just don't have a house to put it in." How perceptive of that child.

Our home should be a trauma center for the whole family. We don't have to be perfect at home—just forgiven and forgiving. We can grow, we can make mistakes, we can shout for joy, we can cry, we can agree, and we can disagree. Home is a place where happy experiences occur. It's a shelter from the problems of the world, a place where love happens, acceptance is given, and security provided.

Home offers a respite from the tragedies that seem to plague the world outside our door, as recounted on the newscasts. Within our four walls we can offer a place of peace.

What can we do as moms to have a home like God intended? As with everything in life, when something is broken we go back to the instruction manual—in our case, the Bible.

The home is God's invention. He designed the home to be the foundation of our society, a place to meet the mental, spiritual, physical, and emotional needs of people. The members of a family must work together to make their home a true home—not just a place where they hang out.

John Henry Jowett says, "The Bible does not say very much about homes; it says a great deal about the things that make them. It speaks about life and love and joy and peace and rest. If we get a house and put these into it, we shall have secured a home."

Prayer

Father God, through Your inspiration and guidance we are turning our house into a home. It's so cozy, warm, comfortable, loving, and such a wonderful place for rest. Thanks for helping to shape our dwelling. Amen.

Action

Continue to seek God's direction in building your home.

The Blankie

Peace I leave with you; My peace I give to you;
not as the world gives do I give to you.
Do not let your heart be troubled, nor let it be fearful.

—JOHN 14:27

When our first grandchild was born, her parents named her Christine Marie—Christine from her mother's middle name and Marie from my middle name. As my namesake I'm very proud of Christine Marie. She is our only granddaughter among four grandsons.

From flannel fabric I made her a piece of pink-printed blanket with some small roses. The blanket was edged with a pink satin binding. It was only about eight inches by eight inches, very small. Well, it quickly became her security blankie while she sucked her thumb. The blankie got twisted, wadded up, and smoothed by little Christine Marie. She was finally able to pull loose an end and twist the threads around her fingers.

Christine loved her pink rosebud blankie. It gave her comfort when she wasn't feeling well, softness when she was afraid, and security when she felt alone. Then one day five years later the blankie got folded and put in an envelope that she tucked away in her dresser drawer. From time to time she still pulls out the envelope to look at the rosebud flannel security blanket.

Jesus is like the security blanket that Christine Marie once held close to her—only today she has almighty God our Heavenly Father, God the Son, and God the Holy Spirit to hold tight to.

As today's Scripture states, Jesus gives us peace in the midst of the storms of life; when we are going through that difficult tornado of a broken marriage, the death of a dream, financial troubles, childless pain, ill health, or all the other trials we encounter in just living out our daily lives.

Christ is our security blanket when we are afraid and feel fearful of tomorrow.

My mama used to tell me in the middle of the night when I needed to go to the bathroom but was afraid of the dark, "Be afraid, but go anyway." Today I know I can go because I have my Lord who is with me wherever I go. When I'm weak and upset, He holds me and comforts my heart.

Of course, Jesus is more than just a security blanket. He's our Comforter, our Savior, the Messiah, the Alpha and Omega, the Almighty, the Everlasting, our bright and morning star, our Counselor, our strength, our Redeemer, our peace, our High Priest, our cornerstone, our foundation, our master builder, and a hundred other necessities for us.

It's time to give our blanket over to Jesus and allow Him to be our Master Comforter. Christine Marie's blankie is now in a beautiful frame, hanging on the wall in her bedroom as a treasured memory of her childhood.

Prayer

Father God, thank You for letting me put away my old childhood security blanket and for giving me faith to trust You in all situations. Amen.

Action

Thank God for the times He has comforted you.

The Lost Mitt

And the LORD will continually guide you,
And satisfy your desire in scorched places,
And give strength to your bones;
And you will be like...a spring of water
whose waters do not fail.

—ISAIAH 58:11

It was my son Brad's first real leather baseball mitt. Bob had taught him how to break it in with special oil to form the pocket just right for catching the ball. The oil was rubbed into the pocket of the glove. Then Brad tossed his baseball from hand to hand to form a pocket just right for him. Brad loved his mitt and worked for hours each day to make it fit just right. He was so happy to have such a special glove for his baseball practice and games.

One afternoon after practice one of the older boys asked to see Brad's mitt. He looked it over, then tossed it away into the grassy field. Brad ran to find his special possession, but he couldn't find it. Nowhere was his mitt to be found. With a frightened, hurt heart, Brad came home in tears.

After telling me the story, I encouraged him by saying that the mitt is there someplace and let's go look. "But Mom, I did search the lot, and it's not there," replied Brad, in tears.

So I said, "Brad, let's pray and ask God to help us." By now it was beginning to get dark and we needed to hurry, so we jumped into the car. As I drove to the baseball field, we asked God to please guide our steps directly to the exact spot where the glove was. After parking, we quickly headed for the field. Again we asked God to point us in the right direction. Immediately Brad ran into the tall grass of the field and there, about 20 feet away, was Brad's glove.

God answers our prayers. Sometimes it's "wait," "yes," or "later." For Brad that day it was a yes. God said in essence, "I'll direct you to find the mitt of this young boy whose heart was broken because of a bully and a lost glove."

Do you have a "lost glove" today? Go before God and praise Him for the promise He gave us in Isaiah 58:11. If God says it, believe it. He will direct you and guide you. Open your heart to listen to what His direction is, then press ahead. The grass may seem too tall for you to see very far, but trust the Lord and keep walking until you feel in your heart the peace you desire. God may lead in a direction you least expect, but step forward with confidence in the Lord.

Prayer

Father God, what an encouragement to me that You care about the smallest details of my life. I do want to be a spring of water to those around me. Amen.

Action

Be specific in your prayers.

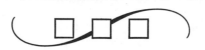

Pray While They're Young

He has given heed to the voice of my prayer.

—Psalm 66:19

Depending on how old your children are, you will soon learn the power of prayer, if you haven't already. As Abraham Lincoln said, "I have been driven many times to my knees by the overwhelming conviction that I had nowhere else to go. My own wisdom, and that all about me, seemed insufficient for the day."

As my children got older, my prayer life became stronger. Somehow children bring parents to their knees—especially as those children go through their teen years. During these awkward years there are so many things that we can't control. Cutting the "apron strings" is very difficult, particularly for us moms.

Somehow dads seem to handle these times a lot better. I remember how cool my Bob would stay during very difficult situations. I often commented under my breath that for him to maintain such composure, he surely must not understand the problem.

I always thanked God when I heard the kids pull in the driveway at night. Then I knew they were safe. When those little "bundles of joy" were young, they were so much fun—but as teenagers, they turned into reasons to pray.

Don't wait until they're older to pray diligently for your children. Every day ask God to guide them, draw them to Him, and keep them safe.

Prayer

God, thank You for [each child's name]. I love this wonderful human being You have given me to mother. Remind me daily to keep my children bathed in prayer. Help me be the exact mother they need. Amen.

Action

Make a short written prayer list for each of your children, listing your top few prayer concerns about each one. Also list the qualities in your child for which you're especially thankful.

Mail a greeting card to each of your children telling them how much you love them. Kids love to get mail, even from Mom, who lives in the same house.

Paying Too Much for a Whistle

...who sold his own birthright for a single meal.
—Hebrews 12:16

$\mathcal{O}$ne of our great Americans, Ben Franklin, tells a little story about a whistle. It brings home the common sense of *not selling one's birthright*. You've often heard that "common sense" is not so common anymore—and how true that is.

When Ben was only seven, he was charmed by the whistle of a friend and impetuously traded all the pennies he had to his friend for this noisemaker. His purchase made him the target of his family and friends, who pointed out to him the folly of bargaining before reflecting on the worth of one's purchase.

In our lives we run across a lot of whistles for sale. Our "common sense" question is, "Are we paying too much for the whistle?" This is especially true when it comes to trading our reputation for a trinket. If former president Clinton had asked himself this question, he might have realized that the price of the whistle named Monica Lewinsky was too much, and he would not have chosen to pay the price he did.

I know of a childless couple who are determined to adopt a baby at any price. A doctor, whom they do not know, heard of their desire, told them of a case in another state in which he could get a child for them providing they would pay the mother's hospital bill, pay him a fat fee, and pay his attorney an equal amount. Are they paying too much for the whistle? Maybe so. Maybe not.

Another woman has a husband who travels a lot, and she has become bored with her lifestyle. A very nice gentleman friend helped her break up her boredom by taking her out to dinner and the movies. What had been a casual occasion has now become a regular occurrence. Is she paying too much for the whistle?

What is a whistle worth? As Christian women we must use the Word of God to help us determine the value of the whistles in our lives. Many times we must answer, "That whistle isn't worth the asking price."

Prayer

Father God, when we find ourselves looking to the future because we aren't content with today, may You give us a peace of mind that lets us rest where You have placed us. Amen.

Action

Tell the story of Ben Franklin's whistle to your children tonight. After you share a time when you paid too much for the whistle, ask them if they can think of a time when they have done the same.

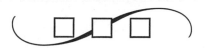

Stars Began to Dance

For you will go out with joy
And be led forth with peace;
The mountains and the hills will break forth
into shouts of joy before you,
And all the trees of the field will clap their hands.

—ISAIAH 55:12

Ideals are like stars. You will not succeed in touching
them with your hands; but, like the seafaring man,
you choose them as your guides, and, following them,
you will reach your destiny. —CARL SCHURZ

One of the great joys of summer is vacation time with the
family—and one of our favorite memory makers was a
recent trip to Idaho. That famous potato state abounds with
unspoiled beauty—majestic mountains, sparkling rivers,
lush vegetation. Many places, in fact, look much as they
did hundreds of years ago.

We had a wonderful time—fishing and hiking, roasting
wieners over a crackling fire, and camping out under the
wide sky. At night, as the sky darkened and the stars began
to dance, we literally could hear God's creation shouting
with joy and clapping her hands. It sounded like lapping

water, singing breezes, chirping insects, and clean, deep silence.

Since then, wherever I am, I try to listen more carefully to the joyful voices of creation all around me—a dancing sea breeze, a purring cat, a rustling clump of desert grass. All these sounds bless me—they remind me of just how good the Creator is, and they inspire me to sing along with the great classic, "How Great Thou Art."

Prayer

Father God, as I gaze into the sky I see You as the Creator of all. Each sight reminds me that You are God and gives evidence to me that You exist. Amen.

Action

Take your children and walk to a quiet part of your neighborhood and look and listen for God's creation. Have each child, along with yourself, write down what you saw and heard. Take every opportunity to teach your children how to appreciate God's glorious creation.

Weeds Aren't Allowed in My Garden

...his enemy came and sowed tares
[weeds] among the wheat...

—MATTHEW 13:25

*M*y Bob loves to garden. Every opportunity he has, he's out in the yard cutting here, planting there, hoeing this, cultivating that. But in all this work, weeds are clearly his biggest challenge! He has a patch of nut grass that won't go away. These rascally weeds have roots that grow horizontally and choke out all neighboring flowers.

Bob has discovered that in a short time, a beautiful section of your yard can be destroyed if you aren't diligent. You can control weeds as they appear above ground—but not their seeds.

Some weed seeds are still able to germinate after being underground for many years. They seemingly lie in wait to germinate at just the right time to choke the life from any nearby domestic plant.

Not only are weed problems part of our gardening experience, but we have weeding problems inside ourselves. While we're casually living life, an enemy comes and seeds

127

our lives with tares. That's what Jesus was talking about in the parable from which today's verse is taken.

The trouble with tares is that they are so like wheat one has trouble in distinguishing between the two. In the parable, it was nearly impossible to pluck out the tares without uprooting the wheat.

When the wrong seeds come into our lives, we have to get rid of them before they germinate and confuse us—contaminating the harvest that God has in mind for us. If you aren't sure of which is the right and which is the wrong, ask God to help you sort it out.

Prayer

Father God, let me be aware of seeds that will become weeds in my life or the lives of my children. Help us uproot spiritual weeds the first moment they crop up. Amen.

Action

Evaluate your life to see if there are things there that should be watched. Watch for any weeds.

God Provides

*Do not be afraid, for am I in God's place? As for you, you
meant evil against me, but God meant it for good
in order to bring about this present result....*

—Genesis 50:19-20

The story of Joseph and his family, which begins in Genesis 37, is a terrific example of how God provides for those who trust in Him. In a brief summary: Jacob favored his son Joseph. Extremely jealous, his brothers plotted against Joseph and after a narrow escape with death, he was sold into slavery. But God was with Joseph. He ended up in Egypt as a trusted servant of Pharaoh who appointed him as overseer of the grain.

Later, during a horrible famine, Jacob sent his sons to Egypt to buy grain and Joseph recognized his brothers, but they didn't recognize him.

In today's Scripture, we hear Joseph's words as he reveals himself to his brothers. Joseph's wisdom is very similar to Paul's encouragement in Romans 8:28, which says, "God causes all things to work together for good to those who love God, to those who are called according to His purpose."

Yes, we mothers can trust God that even evildoers play a part in developing us into whom God wants us to become.

Trust Him for every event in your life—and in the life of each of your children.

Usually when we ask, "Why?" we should be asking, "Why not?" God is a planner for future events. Certain events must take place before other events take place. We are to trust that God's ways are bigger than our ways and that His thoughts are bigger than our thoughts.

God never makes mistakes.

Prayer

Father God, let me trust You more in all the circumstances of life. May You work all things together for good for me and every one of my children. Amen.

Action

Think back over time and recall how God has provided for you, perhaps in a time when you couldn't see how the situation could possibly work out the way it did. Thank God for these events.

Too Much to Do?

...we hear that some among you are leading an undisciplined life, doing no work at all, but acting like busybodies.

—2 THESSALONIANS 3:11

Too many things on your "to-do" list today? Are you overwhelmed with children, house, husband, laundry, meal preparation, work, marketing, and all the multitude of things it takes to run your life?

Has your pursuit of the daily routine left you with no prayer time, no time for Bible study, or no time for even just a few moments of quiet reflection? I know what it's like when that which your heart craves—fellowship with God—just doesn't seem to fit in the schedule. And yet the busier we are, the more we need to be spiritually fit to meet the day's demands.

As a young mom with five children under five, it was difficult for me to put God first, but when I did, my days went so much better. I was able to have a peaceful heart and a sweet spirit, and it was much more likely that the priorities of my day fell into place after even a brief time with the Lord.

Today with grown children and five grandchildren, I can see even more clearly what's really important in life. It's that quiet time when we get to know God's Word, pray God's Word, and walk in God's Word and His promises.

Prayer

Father God, make me aware of the important issues of life. Make my desire to be with You a reality. I truly want to be a mom for God. Amen.

Action

Make a "to-do" list that has reading God's Word at the top of the list.

A Friend Closer
Than a Sister

...there is a friend who sticks closer than a brother.

—PROVERBS 18:24

According to an old Aesop fable, one day a mouse happened to run across the paws of a sleeping lion and awakened him. The lion, angry at being disturbed, grabbed the mouse and was about to swallow him when the mouse cried out, "Please, kind sir, I didn't mean it. If you will let me go, I shall always be grateful, and perhaps I can help you someday."

The idea that such a little thing as a mouse could help him so amused the lion that he let the mouse go. A week later the mouse heard the lion roaring loudly. He went closer to see what the trouble was and found his lion caught in a hunter's net. Remembering his promise, the mouse began to gnaw the ropes of the net and kept it up until the lion could get free. The lion then acknowledged that little friends might prove to be great friends.

I often wonder why some people are attracted to others as friends. Is it because of common interests, past experiences, physical attractions, having children that are friends with another family's children, or attending the same

134 • *Minute Meditations for Busy Moms*

church? What is it that bonds some people together in friendship?

As I consider my many friends, I sense it's a little of all the above. My friends come from various backgrounds, religions, economic levels, nationalities and races, and educational achievement.

There does seem to be one common strand that runs throughout most of my friendships. The majority of us have a kindred spirit in the Lord. So I've determined that friends and friendships are unique gifts of God. Of the friendship with David and Jonathan, it's said that God "knit their hearts together." What an apt description of what happens when you find yourself developing a new friendship.

But as important as friends are, the writer of today's proverb gives us a warning in the first part of verse 24: "A man of too many friends comes to ruin." When I first read that, I was confused. I thought to myself, *I thought we were to have a lot of friends, so why this warning?* But as I considered it, a thought came to me. He was stressing that *too* many friends chosen indiscriminately will bring trouble, but a genuine friend sticks with you through thick and thin. When we use this criterion for a friend, we begin to thin the acquaintance ranks down to those who are truly first-level friends.

I know without a doubt that many of my friends would be and have been with me no matter what the circumstances, what day of the week, or what time of day or night I needed help. I call these my "2 A.M. friends." Every mom needs at least a couple of these valuable friends.

As in the Aesop story, you never know when you will need a friend. I have found that those who have friends are themselves friendly. They go out of their way to be a friend. In order to have friends, one must be a friend.

Prayer

Father God, You have given me some wonderful friends. I would not be who I am without the influence of these dear ladies. I thank You for who they are to me. Amen.

Action

Write a friend a note thanking them for being your friend.

Friendship is unnecessary, like philosophy, like art.... It has no survival value; rather it is one of those things that give value to survival. —C. S. LEWIS

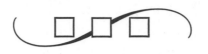

Do You Love Me?

… Jesus said to Simon Peter…
"Do you love Me more than these?"

—JOHN 21:15

$\mathcal{S}$ometimes we go through periods when we wonder if our husbands, our children, and our friends love us. During these times, we feel insecure about the other people in our lives, not sure where we stand with them. Even though we tell and show them that we love them, they seem to want to test that love. Especially our children.

Children may test our love by wearing crazy clothes, putting rings in their body parts, getting tattoos, coloring their hair strange colors, using foul language, or through open disobedience.

In our passage today, Jesus asks Peter three times whether the disciple really loves Him. I believe that these basic questions correspond to Peter's three denials of Jesus (John 13:38). Jesus, in His great love, wanted to give Peter a second chance to follow Him. He didn't want Peter to go all through life with the stigma of denying Jesus. He wanted Peter to know that he was forgiven for his wrong-doing, and he could have a valuable ministry in spreading the gospel through the world.

But before Peter was able to confirm his love for Jesus, Jesus told him in John 21:18-19 that the decision was going to cost him a price. In fact, according to church tradition, Peter and his wife were crucified upside down approximately 40 years later. After stating there would be a price for following Him, Jesus said, "Follow Me," and Peter did.

Yes, love has its cost—not always to the extreme of Peter's—but a cost of time, energy, commitment, money, and devotion. Selfish people take without giving back, but a true lover of people is always giving and giving and giving without asking anything in return.

Is there someone in your life who is asking this basic question: "Do you love me?"

Prayer

Father God, let my words become alive to those around me. Let them know that I truly love them dearly, and that they don't have to test my love to get my attention. Amen.

Action

Seek out those who are asking, "Do you love me?" and assure them that you do.

≈≈≈≈≈≈≈≈≈≈≈≈

Eight Ways to Say I Love You
to Someone You Care About
(Friends, Spouses, Anyone!)

1. Tell them. The words may sound awkward and you may feel a bit silly, but just tell them, "Hey, I know I don't say it often, but you're an important part of my life."
2. Drop a note in the mail that just says hi. Don't mention anything about your difficulties this week, just encourage the person you're writing.
3. Whenever something reminds you of someone, share it with them. Fax them a cartoon, E-mail them an article, call to tell them about a show you thought they'd like to see.
4. Grab your colored markers and start writing all the reasons you care about him or her. "I love you because..." and list silly things as well as the serious ones.
5. Do something they don't like to do or pay to have it done. Iron his shirts; hire a housekeeper for her.
6. Buy twin mugs and tell her/him you will pray for her/him every time that you use yours, wash it, etc.
7. Tell her that you realize s/he goes unappreciated a lot, but you notice all that s/he does and you are grateful.
8. Listen. Turn off the television and ask, "What matters to you? What are your dreams? What can I do to support you as you reach for them?"

—AUTHOR UNKNOWN

A Ten-Day Physical Fitness Program

*Beloved, I pray that in all respects you may prosper
and be in good health, just as your soul prospers.*

—3 JOHN 1:2

Today is the first day of the rest of your life. As a busy mom you are probably stressed by your overall health and appearance. Today is the right time to start shaping up. The following ten-day program will get you started on a spiritual path of rejuvenation. However, I've found that if you're in good spiritual shape you will also be in good physical shape. Try it and see.

First Day: Today I will dine on gratitude—thanking God for the life He gave me and seeing that my "helpings" are generous. I shall share, saying, "Come to the table of the Lord; taste, cherish, enjoy!"

Second Day: Today I will skimp on pessimism, substituting optimism. I shall pray for "sweet things" and know that they will be served!

Third Day: Today I will go on a liquid diet of cheer, sharing a cup of joy with everyone I meet. I shall experiment with flavors of sunshine and song.

Fourth Day: Today I will nibble away until I find something good in each member of my family and friends. I will sift and sort until I find it!

Fifth Day: Today I will drink from the cup of forgiveness—even when the dregs are bitter. I will discard every grudge—no "snacks" allowed!

Sixth Day: Today I will indulge myself in prayer! I have worked very hard on this program and I must rest and ask for new energy.

Seventh Day: Today I will clean my pantry, removing self-pity and selfishness. I have been gluttonous and these must go! Lord, let me not be tempted.

Eighth Day: Today I will discard all of yesterday's leftovers, letting today be sufficient unto itself. A "warmed over" past can spoil my day!

Ninth Day: Today I will serve low-budget "happiness food," remembering that a tender touch, a pleasant smile, a call are great nourishment.

Tenth Day: Today I will fast—refraining from complaint; listening to others.[11]

Prayer

Father God, I so want to get a balanced life. I realize that spiritually I need to work on several areas. Let me begin today. Amen.

Action

Begin with day one—make a list of those things you are thankful for.

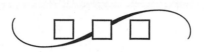

No Harsh Words Allowed

A gentle answer turns away wrath,
But a harsh word stirs up anger.

—PROVERBS 15:1

I just love the Victorian age of history. The Victorians' clothes, hairdos, makeup, and manners enthrall me. Each time I see a good movie set in the latter part of the nineteenth century, my heart longs to return to those days. Back then, women were women and not like the clanging cymbals of today.

I get so unnerved when I hear that certain dress and colors exhibit power in a woman. Where are the days when a woman was known by *who* she was rather than by how much "power" she held over others?

We women all know that inside, a woman can be tranquil like the water on "Golden Pond" or can be a turbulent rapid like Niagara Falls. This is particularly true when we have disagreements with our mates. At those times, we'd do well to heed Solomon's advice in Proverbs 17:14. He says, "The beginning of strife is like letting out water, so abandon the quarrel before it breaks out."

In other words, don't let it start. It's okay to differ with our spouse on an issue, but don't be disagreeable in the process. Keep away from speaking in the flesh. Don't let unwholesome words be uttered. Remember you never have to apologize for words you never said. Always remember that God often speaks to you through your spouse.

Accept your differences of opinion and grow through these episodes. Conflict when done healthily can be a very constructive experience in a marriage. You can disagree without quarreling.

When we catch ourselves disagreeing, we need to exercise the communication skill of listening, which most of us do very poorly. When we listen, we can begin to better understand the other person's point of view. We all need to be better listeners. Learn to have a quiet and gentle spirit.

Prayer

Father God, I needed this today. My spouse and I have been quarreling, and I know that You are not being glorified. Amen.

Action

Stop quarreling and begin to listen.

A Time for Everything

He hath made every thing beautiful in his time.

—ECCLESIASTES 3:11 (KJV)

Ralph Waldo Emerson said it so well:

> Finish every day and be done with it. You have done what you could. Some blunders and absurdities no doubt crept in; forget them as soon as you can. Tomorrow is a new day; begin it well and serenely and with too high a spirit to be cumbered with old nonsense. This day is all that is good and fair. It is too dear, with its hopes and invitations, to waste a moment on yesterday.

Truly there is a season for everything. Behind every happening, there is a purpose. Nothing happens by accident. Life flows through its natural cycles. There is a time to be born, a beginning, and a time to die, an ending. God has a divine timetable.

My mother-in-law recently passed away, and we were richly blessed by knowing that her cycle of life on earth had been completed as God has planned. We knew that through the years, God had turned every ugly event in her life beautiful. And now she was trading her earthly life for one in which there is no more pain.

During her life she had heartaches and laughter, along with sickness and health. There were no "whys" when she passed away. We knew that it was all part of God's cycle for her. When we realize that God has a timing for everything, then we can trust that everything will be beautiful in His perfect time.

Prayer

Father God, You are the Alpha and the Omega. You are the beginning and the end. Let us be patient and learn to live at peace with Your timetable. Let me not rush my agenda. Let me trust You more. Amen.

Action

Wait patiently, and let God's timetable for your life be unfolded.

Listen First

He who gives an answer before he hears,
It is folly and shame to him.

—PROVERBS 18:13

*E*very day we read in the newspaper of people who seem to be crying out, "Listen to me, please! Won't someone please stop and hear my cry?" This is a common request from everyone. We are a country of talkers; very few have the gift of listening.

If you stop and listen very carefully to your conversation at home, your husband and children make the same cry. Oh, it may not be as loud or theatrical as the person in the front-page story, but it is just as real.

When we stop and take time to listen, we are telling the other person, "Your thoughts are important. I care what you think; you have value to me; I want to be involved in your life."

We all have to stop and answer this question, "How good a listener am I?" You will be surprised to know that most of us aren't very good with this skill. If we are to love others, we must be willing to listen to what they have to say. It's impossible to really love someone with the love of God and not be interrupted by their thoughts. Marriage matures and goes up another notch when we are able and willing to listen. Marriages don't grow with deaf ears.

Children sometimes complain that their parents don't listen to them—that they're inaccessible. Do your children say this about you? Are you reachable by your children—or must they constantly seek your attention before they get it? And when you finally are available, do you really listen to them?

Here's a test: Would you be satisfied if God listened to you as intently as you listen to your children when they have an urgent request of you—even if it turns out to be nothing you consider important?

When those moments of true listening occur, you need to stop what you're doing, put down the magazine you're reading, turn off the TV, look into the person's eyes, and let them know they have your fullest attention. Don't even answer the phone during these crucial times.

Prayer

Father God, help me to zip up my mouth when I begin to answer before I listen to find out how the other person yearns to be listened to—especially when it is my child who wants to talk to me. God, You are a parent who is never too busy to listen. May I be the same. Amen.

Action

Refuse to give an answer before you hear all the facts.

Five O'Clock or
Six O'Clock?

*But everyone must be quick to hear, slow to speak,
and slow to anger; for the anger of man does not
achieve the righteousness of God.*

—JAMES 1:19-20

Two of my favorite relatives on my mother's side of the family were Uncle Saul and Auntie Phyllis. For years, whenever they recounted a story they would always disagree on how it happened—they didn't go by boat, they flew; they didn't see the movie, they saw the play; they served chicken, not beef; it was snowing, not sunny. Regardless of the topic they found something to disagree on.

After listening to their squabbles for so long, we'd eventually say, "Five o'clock, six o'clock, what difference does it make?" Yet they would continue to correct each other on the details of the event under discussion. Fortunately they would also smile and laugh and not take it personally, but we knew they would never agree on anything.

Marriage experts tell us that the number one cause for divorce in America today is a lack of communication. This, in spite of the fact that we've all been issued the basic tools for communication at birth—one mouth and two ears. But evidently possessing the physical tools for communication isn't enough. Couples must learn how to use their mouths and ears properly for true communication to take place.

Since God created marriage for companionship, completeness, and communication, we can be sure that He will also provide us with the resources for fulfilling this design.

There are three partners in a Christian marriage: a husband, a wife, and the Holy Spirit. In order for healthy communication to exist between husband and wife, there must be proper communication between all three partners. If there is a breakdown in dialogue between any two members, the breakdown will automatically affect the third member of the triangle.

Dwight Small says, "Lines open to God invariably open to one another, for a person cannot be genuinely open to God and closed to his mate....God fulfills His design for Christian marriage when lines of communication are first opened to Him." If you and your mate are having difficulty communicating, the first area to check is your individual devotional life with God.

Whenever Bob and I suffer a breakdown in relating to one another, it's usually because one of us isn't talking with God on a regular basis. When both of us are communicating with God regularly through prayer and study of His Word, we enjoy excellent communication with each other.

Norm Wright gives an excellent definition of communication: "Communication is a process, either verbal or nonverbal, of sharing information with another person in such a way that they understand what you are saying. Talking and listening and understanding are all involved in the process of communication."

Effective communication between a husband and wife has a fringe benefit—your children also will learn to be good communicators. On the other hand, if your connection with your husband is poor, theirs likely will be also. Make sure that the communication they witness between you and your husband is genuine, loving, and respectful. Someday their mates will thank you for modeling for them this secret of a happy marriage.

Prayer

Father God, since You gave me two ears, let me listen twice as much as I speak. Amen.

Action

Spend more time listening and understanding than talking.

Always Means Always

*[Love] always protects, always trusts,
always hopes, always perseveres.*

—1 CORINTHIANS 13:7 NIV

Sometimes it's hard for us mere mortals to understand adequately the word "always." In today's culture we don't understand love as that kind of commitment. When we say "always," don't we usually mean "sometimes"...or "most of the time"? But "always " really means eternal and everlasting. Can we really commit to *always*?

When God through Scripture says "always," it means "always"—no exception. Never changing, dependable for eternity. I am challenged when Paul says that love

> *Always* protects
> *Always* trusts
> *Always* hopes
> *Always* perseveres

I so want my husband and children to honor me with that kind of love. I want to be a woman who is known for her word: "When Mom says something, you can take it to the bank." In this regard, my advice to moms is, "Just do what you say you are going to do." By so doing, you teach your children the meaning of being trustworthy. You also teach them to trust others—and that's a rare quality in this age of cynicism. But I've learned that he or she who trusts others will make fewer mistakes than the person who distrusts others.

The Living Bible translates Romans 8:24 into, "We are saved by trusting. And trusting means looking forward to getting something we don't yet have—for a man who already has something doesn't need to hope and trust that he will get it."

Moms, we are to be women of integrity. Our word can *always* be trusted. When we are these kind of women, our husband, our children, and our friends will stand at the gate and call us blessed.

Prayer

Father God, I want to be an "always" person. When I say something, I want it always to be true. My friends can say, "If she said it, it must be true." What a great responsibility to be that kind of woman. Amen.

Action

Tell your husband and children that with God's help you will always love them.

How to Love the Rich Life

*For the sun rises with a scorching wind and
withers the grass; and its flower falls off and the beauty
of its appearance is destroyed; so too the rich man
in the midst of his pursuits will fade away.*

—JAMES 1:11

One of our young grandchildren asked Papa Bob, "Are you rich?"

"Yes, in the Lord," he answered.

"No, Papa, I mean *really* rich?" he insisted. He wanted to know if his grandpa was *monetarily* rich. The good old capitalist word: money.

Regardless of where most of us are on the financial barometer of life, we are rich compared to someone—especially when we consider the world's population. Just by living in America we are rich. If you don't think so, just ask any of the many immigrants, legal and illegal, who come to this country every year.

And being rich carries a lot of responsibility. When one is wealthy, that person usually has power over things and people. In 1 Timothy 6:10 we read, "For the love of money is a root of all sorts of evil, and some by longing for it have wandered away from the faith and pierced themselves with many griefs."

The writer isn't saying that being rich is wrong, but that the love of money is the basis for all kinds of evil. We need to examine our attitude toward material wealth. And the result of that examination should determine how we live—because how we live communicates what our concept of wealth is to our children.

A simple lifestyle (as opposed to an ostentatious, wasteful lifestyle) lets our children know that whatever riches we have aren't the most important priority in our life. Instead, let's be good stewards of the gifts God has given us—giving generously to others in need, both of our time and our financial resources. And bring your children into discussions about how and where to give to others.

Exhibit that your security and peace doesn't come from your bank account, but from your relationship with Christ. Live in such a way that your children will understand that your riches in heaven are more exciting than your riches on earth. Teach them that it's more blessed to give than to receive.

Prayer

Father God, You are a provider of abundance. May our family be found worthy to be a steward of all Your resources. I thank You for the riches You have given us. Amen.

Action

Plan to increase your giving to God's worthy causes. Make 1 Timothy 6:10 a family memory verse. Write it out on a 3x5 card and have each family member learn it by heart.

Minister to Those Who Minister!

*For God is not unjust so as to forget your work and
the love which you have shown toward His name,
in having ministered and in still ministering to the saints.*

—HEBREWS 6:10

The well-known author A.C. Dixon told the story of Johanna Ambrosius, the wife of a poor farmer who lived in the German Empire during the latter part of the nineteenth century. She and her husband spent many long hours in the fields, so she knew little of the outside world. But the Lord had given Johanna the soul of a poet.

With her hope in God, she wrote beautiful poems from the thoughts that filled her heart. Through her art, she expressed her great sympathy for the struggling people around her. Her mother's heart toward her people told their stories and sorrow through the arduous life they led.

Somehow, a bit of verse she had written found its way into print and, later, into the hands of the Empress of Germany. The royal lady was so impressed by the beauty of what she read that she asked that the author be located. Learning of Johanna and her meager lifestyle, the Empress expressed her love for the woman by supplying her immediate needs and by giving her a pension for life.

While conducting a seminar in a small town in central Georgia, I noticed a particular man who was really working hard on a late Friday afternoon to make the church just right for the 400 ladies coming to the Saturday women's conference. I was very impressed by how diligently he worked, so I went up to him and asked, "What do you do around here?"

His response was classic. He stated, "No one knows until I don't do what they think I should do."

There are many such unheralded workers in our churches. We need to tell these men and women who labor in obscurity that they are important to the body of Christ. God observes everything a person does to help bear the burden of others— and He will reward him or her. His eternal pension is guaranteed. Remember, God sees each of our labors of love.

> Work is the natural exercise and function of man....Work is not primarily a thing one does to live, but the thing one lives to do. It is, or should be, the full expression of the worker's faculties, the thing in which he finds spiritual, mental, and bodily satisfaction, and medium in which he offers himself to God.
>
> —DOROTHY L. SAYERS

Prayer

Father God, let me have a tender heart to those servants who minister to the body of Christ. Amen.

Action

Tell someone today who is serving in obscurity that you appreciate their hard work. Teach your children that they should never be unwilling to do even the smallest task that God calls them to do.

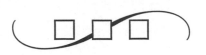

Being Passed Over

For not from the east, nor from the west,
Nor from the desert comes exaltation;
But God is the Judge;
He puts down one and exalts another.

—PSALM 75:6-7

*N*othing hurts like being passed over in life when you felt like you should have been selected for the team, chosen for the lead in the play, elected president of the club, or perhaps loved by that handsome football player you had a crush on in high school.

Today's verse is for all of us bypassed people who have felt left out. We all have wanted a certain position and didn't get it. We all have felt the sting of rejection, and there's perhaps only one thing more painful—watching our children be passed over for something on which they've set their heart.

At such times, Mom is the one to whom they turn for consolation. You'll be called on to give them the necessary lesson in how to have a stiff upper lip in times of disappointment.

The wise mother will point her disappointed child to this powerful verse that tells us that man isn't the one to exalt, but God is the Judge of who gets exalted. Lifting up isn't from the east, the west, or even the south. *God will lift up in His time, not ours.*

This is a hard life principle to learn, but ever so valuable, because God knows our hearts and yet is always wise in His decisions. He will give us the recognition we need in due season. For right now, it's someone else's turn, and it will speed your children's healing if they can learn to rejoice with those who rejoice.

Their day will come and it will be even sweeter for them, knowing that God has chosen the time for them to be picked.

Prayer

Father God, take from me the desire for earthly recognition. Let me focus on the task, not on the reward. I know that You will lift me up in Your time—I trust You for that. Help me be a supportive mom when the time comes for me to comfort my child when he or she has been passed over. Amen.

Action

Uproot from your heart any desire to seek man's recognition. Be there for your child during times of rejection.

Silence Is Powerful

But Jesus made no further answer; so Pilate was amazed.
—MARK 15:5

How often have you thought to yourself, *Oh, if only I would have remained silent!* I know I've certainly wished I could take back my words, words either spoken in anger or in hasty judgment. As a result of those painful times, I'm learning that silence is one of the greatest virtues of the Christian lifestyle.

A Welsh writer of the last century, Mrs. Jessie Penn-Lewis, commenting on the silence of Jesus, said that the Christian who is living close to the Lord will manifest humility and self-control even under the most trying circumstances. She wrote:

> We will be silent in our lowly service among others, not seeking to be "seen of men." Silent while we stoop to serve the very ones who betrayed us. Silent when forced by others to some position where apparent rivalry with another much-abused servant of God seems imminent, only to be hushed by utter self-effacement in our silent withdrawal without explanation, irrespective of our "rights."

As I listen to the news or read the daily paper, I often hear someone referred to as an "activist." Today everyone wants to be vocal about their cause. Usually their thrust is about rights and privileges. Very little is said by these people about responsibilities, accountability, or thankfulness. We seem to be a world of wants and demands.

Even in our personal relationships, we can be full of selfish demands. We can get hurt feelings or feel angry at being neglected. Or we may even be totally correct in our assessment—but wrong in our attitude. And if so, our words of response will betray us as we lash out unkindly toward those we hold responsible.

Perhaps our child will challenge us. We've been "unfair" or we "don't understand" or "everyone else is doing it." When we respond with emotional words of anger, we find ourselves entangled in an argument that can only produce more tension and bruised feelings.

Often the best response is to say nothing. An argument can only progress when someone responds. Remember, it takes two to tangle. If no response is given, then the argument or disagreement dies because of lack of words. If you're tempted to speak in anger or judgment, it's time to follow Jesus' example and "make no further answer."

Words unsaid are usually the best kind.

Prayer

Father God, I appreciate Your example of often saying few words. I really want that to be my response. Give me the proper nudging to keep quiet. Help me not to hurt my children by raising my voice in anger to them. Amen.

Action

Be quiet when your boiling level is raised and you want to speak your piece.

Sure Cure–Prayer

...be reconciled to your brother...
—Matthew 5:24

While looking through an antique store in Georgia, I ran across an old, framed stitchery sampler that was titled "Sure Cure." It went like this:

> Ingredients: One pound of resolution, two grains of common sense, two ounces of experience, 12 ounces of dislike, one large sprig of time, three quarts of cooling water, and a great quantity of consideration.
>
> Directions: Set these over the gentle fire of love, sweeten with the sugar of forgetfulness, skim with the spoon of melancholy. Put the best inside, cook it with the conscience, let it remain, and you will find quick ease to restore sense.
>
> These articles can be had at the apothecary's, at the home of Understanding, next door to Reason, on Prudent Street, in the Village of Contentment, built on Prayer. This is the sure-cure for the disease, "We Never Speak as We Pass By."

How easy it is to let hard feelings, misunderstandings, and fake expectations divide relationships. The callousness of a hard heart can destroy all the love we once had for a loved one. This breakdown in communication will destroy a sweet fellowship, and it will eventually affect your communion with God. Prayer is the vital ingredient of Christian health. Prayer brings us closer to God and to others.

Prayer

Father God, the sure cure of prayer brings us back to a lost relationship. Today I commit all my rifts to You. Heal my heart so I will have loving forgiveness. Amen.

Action

If you have any petty differences with a friend or family member, bring them to the Lord in prayer.

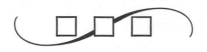

Be a Cheerleader

[Love] bears all things, believes all things,
hopes all things, endures all things.

—1 CORINTHIANS 13:7

Both my daughter, Jenny, and my granddaughter, Christine, have been high school cheerleaders. Ever since I can remember we have had pom-poms in the house. I remember the many days that the other cheerleaders gathered at our house to practice their routines. Hours and hours of exhausting rehearsals went into every Friday night game.

As I think back over these years, I reflect on the time and energy both girls devoted to rooting for their team. And now, all these years later, I realize that all those many hours of cheerleading were great training for marriage. For as wives and mothers, one of our privileges is to be cheerleaders for our husbands and children. The team we now root for consists of one man—the captain of the team—and the members of the team—the children.

Anne Morrow Lindbergh, the wife of the famous aviator, Charles Lindbergh, acted as a cheerleader for her husband—and he for her. As she once said:

> To be deeply in love, of course, is a great liberating
> force and the most common experience that frees....

Ideally, both members of a couple in love free each other to new and different worlds. I was no exception to the general rule. The sheer fact of finding myself loved was unbelievable and changed my world, my feelings about life and myself. I was given confidence, strength, and almost a new character.[12]

Have you freed those you love to be all that God wants them to be? Given them the confidence to step out and trust God with their lives? Mom, you become the cheerleader for your family. Someday your husband and children will stand at the gate and call you blessed. Be an encourager. Hip-Hip-Hooray!!

Prayer

Father God, I get so excited about cheering for my family. Lift me up daily to find the best in them. I pray that they can believe in themselves. Amen.

Action

Give each of your family members one word of encouragement today.

Behold, Your Mother

Then He said to the disciple, "Behold, your mother!"
—JOHN 19:27

*B*eholding one's mother is one of the greatest honors one could bestow on a woman. I realize there are some readers who have not had pleasant experiences with their mothers. However, the position of motherhood is one that should be honored. If you had a good mother, "praise the Lord"; if not, then you become the mother that you wished you'd had.

One of my favorite mothers is Sarah Edwards. She was one of the great women in American history. She had a great influence upon her family even extending to future generations. Sarah was married to the famous theologian, Jonathan Edwards. The couple were the parents of 11 children. It was the responsibility of Sarah to raise those children, and it was a job she took on with great passion!

At the same time, Sarah maintained a vital, loving relationship in her marriage to Jonathan. How did she do it all? After all, she only had 24 hours in a day, just like us. As a deeply Christian woman, Sarah was a firm, patient mother who treated her children with courtesy and love. She was able to guide her children without angry words or temper outbursts. She had only to speak once and her children obeyed her. They had learned to respect their parents, obey God, and always exhibit good manners.

Sarah is one whom we can respect as an expert manager of her colonial home. She wasn't blessed with all the gadgets we have today. She would have loved our microwave ovens, dishwashers, and vacuum cleaners.

Even with her heavy schedule, Sarah made spending time with her Lord her top priority. This gave her strength to fulfill her daily "to-do" list. The Edwards' descendants included

13 college presidents
65 college professors
100 lawyers
30 judges
66 physicians
80 holders of public office
3 U.S. Senators
3 mayors of large cities
3 state governors
1 vice-president of the United States
1 comptroller of the U.S. Treasury Department

All Sarah's work as a mother paid great dividends. Her descendants would truly rise up and call her blessed. I wonder, will ours?

Prayer

Father God, give me a mentor from whom I can learn. Modeling is so very important. I'm looking for a good road map. Please send me a godly woman to learn from. Amen.

Action

When you see a good mother in action—whether at church or while out shopping—honor her by complimenting her on her well-behaved children.

We Need Poor Richard's Almanac

The wise woman builds her house,
But the foolish tears it down with her own hands.
—PROVERBS 14:1

More than 200 years after he wrote it, Benjamin Franklin's *Poor Richard's Almanac* is as full of wisdom as the day it was written. Ben Franklin used the *Almanac* as a way of teaching the early colonists how to be frugal. These early readers needed to know some basic principles in order to survive living off the land's natural resources.

Even though times have changed from rural to urban life for most of us, Franklin's philosophy is still useful. A few of his guiding principles:

* A good example is the best sermon.
* Who pleasure gives, shall joy receive.
* A long life may not be good enough, but a good life is long enough.
* Great beauty, great strength, and great riches are really and truly of no great use; a right heart exceeds all.

* Content makes poor men rich; discontent makes rich men poor.
* Who is rich? He that rejoices in his portion.
* Search others for their virtues, thyself for thy vices.
* The doors of wisdom are never shut.

Prayer

Father God, You are awesome. You are the giver of all wisdom; our most acceptable service that we can render to You is by doing good to Your other children. Amen.

Action

It's not likely that your children will study the wise words of Ben Franklin in school. Tonight read aloud a few of his guiding principles and ask your children to make up some wise sayings about life. Print them on a sheet of paper and post the page on the refrigerator along with Ben Franklin's admonitions.

Every Job Is Significant

Whatever you do, do your work heartily,
as for the Lord rather than for men.

—Colossians 3:23

As a burned-out mom, do you get discouraged when no one in the family seems to appreciate all the endless things you do for them? I know I did—until one day I realized I was trying to serve the wrong people. I switched tactics and began to work heartily for the Lord rather than for man. My expectations turned completely around—my goal was to serve and be a witness to those to whom I ministered.

If sometimes your work seems like a waste of time, then maybe you could begin to consider your work (either in or out of the home) as a place of ministry—then perform your duty as if you were doing it for Jesus. He's the One you're really serving.

"Why do I do what I do? Is it to please man or God?" These two questions we must answer ourselves because how we answer reveals how we look at life. If we work to please people, we will never be satisfied because people always expect more from us, and we can never give enough. If we work to please God, then we will hop out of bed each morning to see what the new day brings.

Perhaps if we take up this challenge, we can profit by listening to John Dodd, who wrote several centuries ago: "Whatsoever our calling be, we serve the Lord Christ in them....They are the most worthy servants...that...serve the Lord, where He hath placed them."

If God's purposes are to be fulfilled, we must not neglect the ordinary tasks in our pursuit of the glorious ones. Meals must be cooked, trash must be collected, assembly lines must be manned, and children must be attended to. Every service done unto God is significant.

Martin Luther once said, "A dairy maiden can milk a cow to the glory of God."

Prayer

Father God, may I want to serve You rather than man. Let my joy be complete in You! I only need Your praises. Amen.

Action

Go out and milk a cow to the glory of God.

Love Your Neighbors

...you shall love your neighbor as yourself.
—MATTHEW 22:39

*O*ver the past many years we have had some wonderful neighbors who have added so much joy to our lives. In many cases they have been as close as family.

Our lives would be very lonely without neighbors. With good neighbors, we likewise strove to be good neighbors. Due to my recent illness, we have had to move closer to my oncologist. For the first time in 16 years we have become the new people on the block. Where we were always the welcomer, we now have become ones who are being welcomed.

What a pleasant experience it has been. Many of those in the neighborhood had been told about my illness and that I was a Christian writer and speaker. Some of the women had even read my books and attended my seminars. They were marvelous. Food arrived, floral arrangements appeared, dinner invitations were extended, errands were offered to be run; they all were concerned that we had a proper welcome. The men even offered Bob the use of their tools if needed.

There's so much to the "good neighbor policy." And it all begins with love. God tells us to love our neighbor. And a good mother is a good neighbor.

Prayer

Father God, thank You for giving us such wonderful neighbors. They have so enriched our lives. May I live out Your command to love my neighbors. Amen.

Action

Be a good neighbor by keeping your yard mowed and kept up. No one likes to live next door to an eyesore.

Mary, Martha, and Me

...Mary has chosen the good part,
which shall not be taken away from her.

—LUKE 10:42

*T*he age-old story of hardworking Martha versus the more spiritually sensitive Mary truly illustrates the dilemma of today's busy mom.

For a long time, I've been more like Martha than Mary. Although I really desire to be more like Mary, my Martha side keeps getting in the way.

When company is on the way, my Martha side says, "I've been waiting for this special guest in my home, and I want it to be clean and in order." So I can sympathize with Martha who, when Jesus was coming, worked so hard to make everything just right, only to feel abandoned by Mary who, instead of lending a helping hand, left her side to sit at Jesus' feet. Martha needed help to carry this party off, but Mary was preoccupied with Jesus. This made Martha a little impatient.

My Mary side says housework can wait; Jesus is more important. I need to spend my time with Him. I can always tidy up after His journey is over. Martha/Mary/Me says I need a balance in my tidiness and in my passion for other people's needs. Discernment is very important as we try to prioritize our practical and spiritual activities.

Finally, Martha got so upset with Mary that she went to Jesus to complain. But Jesus sided with Mary and said, "Martha, Martha, you are worried and bothered about so many things; but only one thing is necessary, for Mary has chosen the good part, which shall not be taken away from her."

Jesus said that Mary was pleasing Him by paying attention to Him and His situation. The Martha in me nags to keep my house in order each day, but my Mary side says gently, "I need time to pray." Martha is concerned with what neighbors might think if they drop in and find dishes stacked in the kitchen sink. But Mary answers, "Selfish! I think it's a crime if you don't share your talents and time with others."

In truth, both issues must be addressed in our lives. We have to balance out the Martha and Mary sides of our lives so that our Lord is pleased with what we do. For we surely know that if Jesus had asked Mary to get Him a drink of water or some other practical thing, she would have sprung into action.

Prayer

Father God, both Martha's and Mary's voices ring in my ears. Give me the proper perspective so You will be pleased with my balance of life. Amen.

Action

Think about the balancing out of your Martha and Mary dilemma. What changes need to be made?

Restoration

He restores my soul;
He guides me in the paths of righteousness....

—PSALM 23:3

*P*rincess Elizabeth, daughter of Charles I, was found dead one day with her head leaning on the Bible and the Bible open at the words, "Come unto me all ye that labor and are heavy laden, and I will give you rest." Her monument in Newport Church consists of a female figure reclining her head on a marble book, with the above text engraved on the book.

As busy moms you can relate to the notion that you need rest. We are wearing thin mentally, physically, and emotionally by all that we must do each day. Some days we seem to be chasing our tails and going in circles just to keep up with our hectic schedule. Faster, faster, and still we get behind.

How does one get restored? Listen to this wise advice:

> You don't have to be a super mom.
> You don't have to be perfect.
> Accept limitations on what you can do.
> Meet God each day in study and prayer.
> Say "No" to good things and save your "Yes"
> for the best.

Don't sweat the small stuff.
Enjoy the small wonders around you.
God restores you.

Prayer

Father God, You can and do restore my soul. Only through You can I restore my soul. You are my resting place. Amen.

Action

Determine that you are going to be restored. What will you do?

God Gives Comfort

...thy rod and thy staff they comfort me.

—Psalm 23:4 (kjv)

The shepherd protects his sheep with his rod or club (used to fight off wild beasts), and he guides straying sheep with his staff or crook.

The great theologian Charles Spurgeon reflected on this great comfort:

> Give me the comforts of God, and I can well bear the taunts of men. Let me lay my head on the bosom of Jesus, and I fear not the distraction of care and trouble. If my God will give the light of his smile, and glance his benediction, it is enough. Come on foes, persecutors...the Lord God is my sun and shield. I carry a sun within; blow, wind of the frozen north, I have a fire of living coal within; yea death slay me, but I have another life—a life in the light of God's countenance.

Here was a man who knew that Jesus was all he needed. He was secure in his faith and realized that his comfort came from the rod and staff of his Shepherd—Jesus Christ.

Only look at your daily newspaper or TV news and you will realize that we face ongoing problems of violence, life-threatening disease, and political uncertainty.

The challenge of the Christian is to live in the world but not by its standards. To live by the world's standards is to have the world's strength in the day of trouble. No thank you! To live by God's grace is to have God's strength in the day of trouble—that's for me! How about you?

No matter how the world goes, we can be secure in our relationship with our God.

Prayer

Father God, down through the years I have held firmly onto Your rod and staff. You have upheld me in times of weakness. I appreciate the strength and comfort You have given me! Amen.

Action

Come alongside someone who shows signs of weakness and a need for encouragement.

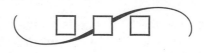

Be a Risk Taker

I can do all things through Him [Jesus] who strengthens me.

—Philippians 4:13

*S*o many of our dreams remain unfulfilled all our life because we aren't willing to take risks to see them come true. I've noticed that the real winners along this road called life are those who are willing to step out in godly faith and step boldly into the unknown.

Today's passage is a wonderful faith builder. Once we realize that we are nothing without Christ and that with Him we can do all things, we begin to see the seemingly impossible become possible. Little did I ever think that God could take me, a high school graduate, a maker of a home with no credentials for writing, and allow me to have the ministry that my husband and I have today.

Only God could make this happen.

When our ministry first started my Bob was a vice president and general manager of a manufacturing company in southern California. During a downturn in our economy, Bob had to close down his business. For the first time in more than 30 years he was unemployed. So, also for the first time, we were able to risk a new beginning. What did we have to lose?

Now, 20 years later we rejoice in what God has done. He opened the door of opportunity through what at the time seemed like a reverse of circumstances, and we walked through. We made mistakes as all dreamers do when they pursue their dream, but through it all, God has given—and still gives us—the strength to go on with our dream.

You may think that as a mom, you don't really have the opportunity to dream dreams or to anticipate taking great risks. But God's not limited by your vocation. Your only limits are those you impose on yourself. Dream big for your life, for your husband, for your children. Teach them what it means to be a risk taker and how to know which risks are worth taking and which are worth passing.

Remember this:

> To laugh is to appear the fool.
> To weep is to risk appearing sentimental.
> To reach out for another is to risk involvement.
> To expose feelings is to risk exposing your true self.
> To place your ideas, your dreams, before the crowd is to risk their loss.
> To love is to risk not being loved in return.
> To live is to risk dying.
> To hope is to risk despair.
> To try is to risk failure.
> But risks must be taken, because the greatest hazard in life is to risk nothing.
> The person who risks nothing, does nothing, has nothing, and is nothing.
> He may avoid suffering and sorrow.
> But he simply cannot learn, feel, change, grow, love, and live.
> Chained by his certitudes, he is a slave.
> He has forfeited freedom.
> Only a person who risks is free.[13]

Prayer

Father God, let me step out in faith and risk adventure in my life. Help me develop the sense of bravery in my children needed by risk takers. And when I see the onset of adverse circumstances, may I discern correctly if it's really a door of opportunity opened for me. With Your help, I know I can do all things. Amen.

Action

Do something today that stretches your risk level. Read the above saying by Norman Wright to your children tonight and discuss its meaning with them. Let them do most of the talking while you listen and simply guide the discussion.

The Dream

The Dream
may be modest or heroic,
vaguely defined or crystal clear,
a burning passion or a quiet guiding force,
a source of inspiration and strength or of corrosive conflict.
My life is enriched to the extent that
I have a Dream and give it appropriate place in my life—
a place that is legitimate and viable
for both myself and my world.
If I have not a Dream or can find no way to live it out my life lacks
genuine purpose or meaning.[14]

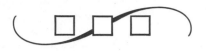

Bless Your Spouse

So then we pursue the things which make for peace and the building up of one another.

—ROMANS 14:19

You would think that "blessing your spouse" would be very easy to do, but my observation is that sometimes it's hard. Marriage partners have to work together to be at peace and to build up one another.

The word "blessing" comes from two Greek words meaning "well" and "word." When you bless your husband, you're literally saying, "I speak well of my spouse."

We bless our mates when we speak well of them, compliment them, and encourage them. That goes for our children also.

Here are some good ways to develop the habit of blessing your mate:

1. Make a decision never to be critical of your partner's thoughts, words, or deeds.

2. Study your mate to learn what makes him tick. Be creative in how you relate to his ticker.

3. Make a list of your husband's positive qualities. Think upon these traits and give his negative qualities to God.

4. Make it a habit to be positive in your comments. Lift him up in private and in public.

5. Let your husband know for sure that you are on the same team as he is. Let him know that you are his biggest fan and his number one supporter.

Prayer

Father God, let me be a blessing to my husband and to my children. I want my spouse to know that I love him and he is my priority for our marriage. I want my children to indeed be blessed. Help me as I try daily to bless them. Amen.

Action

Bless your husband and children today by speaking well of them.

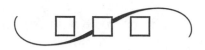

A House Is Built on Wisdom

*By wisdom a house is built, and through understanding
it is established; through knowledge its rooms are
filled with rare and beautiful treasures.*

—PROVERBS 24:3-4 (NIV)

*S*o many moms ask me how to raise a healthy family. I come back with three basic principles of today's Scripture passage. We raise our family with

> Wisdom
> Understanding
> Knowledge

As a result, we've reaped some rare and beautiful treasures—children who are obedient, polite, and considerate and who honor God.

When we're out in public and observe a healthy, functioning family, we know that they directly or indirectly have been observing these three important principles. How do we know that? Because we can see the rewards—children who are a blessing to their parents and to others. These faithful parents have rare and beautiful treasures.

Is it easy then to be so blessed?

No! It takes a lot of hard work and stick-to-it discipline to have these treasures. Plus, you have to believe in the end results.

My Bob and I always go up to the parents of well-behaved children and compliment them on their efforts. We all should praise parents when we see something good. What an encouragement such praise is to the parents. Sometimes parents need to be reminded they're doing an excellent job!

> What the majority of American children needs is to stop being pampered, stop being indulged, stop being chauffeured, stop being catered to. In the final analysis, it is not what you do for your children but what you have taught them to do for themselves that will make them successful human beings.
>
> —ANN LANDERS

Prayer

Father God, give me the desire to raise our children with wisdom, understanding, and knowledge. It would be such a blessing to have all our rooms filled with rare and beautiful treasures. Amen.

Action

Along with your spouse declare that you are going to raise your children with wisdom, understanding, and knowledge.

Lord, Keep Me Safe

*But Peter said to Him, "Even though all
may fall away, yet I will not."*

—Mark 14:29

"Mother," said little Jimmy one morning after having fallen from bed, "I think I know why I fell out of bed last night. It was because I slept too near the place where I got in." Thinking a little more, he corrected himself. "No, that was not the reason; it was because I slept too near to where I fell out."

How often we think that we can pass a test that others have failed. "Oh no, I will never get hooked on drugs," utters a very confident teenager. A young, lonesome wife says with assurance, "Fred is just a friend and I can handle that. There is no romantic entanglement."

Young people are so confident of their strength and their ability to withstand danger. When I need some "grunt work" done around the house, I love to hire some over-confident youths from church. They think they can move a piano all by themselves. The heavier the object, the more assured they are. Give them a positive comment about their strength and they just beam with delight.

Unfortunately, many times in our strength we become weak, and our defenses against temptations fall one by one. We discover we're not immune to the snare of sin after all.

We find ourselves doing things we said we would never do.

Peter, who loved Jesus with great passion, fell by that very passion. "Not I, Master," he said. "Yes, Peter, even you!" the Lord replied.

Yes, Lord, I too can fall unless I trust Your mercy and goodness to keep me safe.

Prayer

Father God, I don't want my strength to become my weakness. Reveal to me those areas of my life where I am weak. Give me a protective hedge to go around me. I need Your armor for safety. Amen.

Action

Identify your weak areas and put a hedge around those areas.

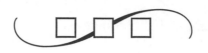

Look Forward, Not Backward

Do not call to mind the former things,
Or ponder things of the past.

—Isaiah 43:18

*H*ave you ever been a prisoner of your past? Have the steel bars of guilt held you captive? Do you break out in sweat when conversation comes out about what you used to be? Do certain triggers set off memories of the life you used to lead?

At one time or another most of us suffer from painful memories of what we were before we became Christians. One thing that I like so much about hearing people give their testimonies is how great the grace of God is. He can take the worst of sinners (which we all have been) and make us white as snow. No social programs, as great as they may be, can change and wash a person's past into the purity of forgiveness.

In 2 Corinthians 5:17 Paul says, "Therefore if anyone is in Christ, he is a new creature; the old things passed away; behold, new things have come." The grace of God not only justifies but also makes "a new creation" which results in a changed life.

Only God can fully satisfy the hungry heart of man.

The greatest challenge of the day is: how to bring about a revolution of the heart, a revolution which has to start with each one of us? When we begin to take the lowest places, to wash the feet of others, to love our brothers with that burning love, that passion, which led to the CROSS, then we can truly say, "Now I have begun."

—DOROTHY DAY

Prayer

Father God, You know how I want to be like You. The deepest part of my heart and soul aches for Your wisdom. May today be a special day for new revelation. Amen.

Action

Forget about your past—God has. Move forward into the future.

And It Was Good

...and God saw that it was good.

—GENESIS 1:10

As moms on the go, we often don't take the time to see, hear, and smell God's creation. We find ourselves being so busy that we don't take the precious time to study God's creation in its fullness.

Do you see evidence of God when you look around you?

As I'm writing, the day is foggy where I live, and I can spy a single drop of dew on the leaves out my kitchen window. With the sun breaking through the fog bank, this little drop of moisture is giving back to God a tiny sparkle of light that He sent from heaven. Dew drops are a marvelous beginning of a cycle that will lead to rain as it drifts eastward across Arizona and New Mexico.

Shakespeare spoke of "a gentle dew from heaven." He too must have taken a pause to look at a droplet of God's creation. He too must have been moved by the wonder of even such a small sample of God's work.

I can fully understand how God, after His work of creation, looked it over and confirmed that it was good. If only we humans, after we create something, could be as satisfied with our work before we move on to another activity or project.

If only we were more concerned about the quality of our work. Our culture hungers for excellence. Those businesses that are able to satisfy that hunger are rewarded by success.

As moms, let's rest between creations. Slow down and wait until the Lord tells us "it is good."

Prayer

Father God, it is so good just to know that You created the droplets left by fog, so good to know You care about the smallest elements of life. Amen.

Action

Look about and see God's creation—be still, oh my soul.

All in the Family

She watches over the affairs of her household....
—PROVERBS 31:27 (NIV)

Women often ask me how to build a strong family. There's not a simple answer to that question. Authors have written entire books attempting to offer the answer, often without arriving at a consensus.

I do know a few things about strong families, though. One is just how important they can be during unexpected adversity. During my recent serious illness the various members of our family have been the force behind my recovery. If I didn't realize it before, I realize it now—family is so very, very important. When all is said and done, family is the most important part of a person's life. Without good family, there wouldn't be as much joy as there is.

I've noticed a few common threads among the strong families I know, and perhaps these might offer some insight.

* All strong families have the ability to express open appreciation and affection—there are a lot of hugs, kisses, and pats on the back. The commonly spoken phrases include "I love you," "You are great," "You add a lot to our family."
* Often the mothers in these families nurture spiritual well-being. Each member seems willing to act as stress

absorbers for others in the family when necessа. Strong families know they're there for each other foг the duration. Family ranks very high on every family member's priority list.

* The strong sense of family manifests itself by a desire to engage in joint activities, rather than going one's own way. Birthdays, anniversaries, holidays, and other important family dates (as well as family history) are big deals. A lot of family photographs are displayed around the home.

* Rewards and awards are often given for the slightest achievements. In our family, recognition was given by using our famed red "You Are Special" plate.

* Genuine spirituality is a family project. Issues are discussed, the Bible is read, prayers are spoken, meals are blessed, the poor remembered.

All these elements help to make healthy families. After all, "as our families go, so goes America."

Prayer

Father God, thank You for the wonderful family You have given me. Each person means so much to me. They give me a reason for living. Amen.

Action

Plan an activity that the whole family would enjoy. Include grandparents.

"100—Good Work"

*...walk in a manner worthy of the Lord,
to please Him in all respects....*

—COLOSSIANS 1:10

A first grader beamed with satisfaction as he handed his parents a spelling test on which his teacher had written a large, "100—Good Work!" The boy later said, "I showed this to Dad and Mom because I knew it would please them."

Can't you just see this little boy riding home on the bus, hardly able to wait for the moment when his parents would express their excitement with how well he had done in school.

A strong desire to please our Heavenly Father is the highest incentive we have for doing His will in our lives. We may have other worthy motives such as the inner satisfaction gained from doing what is right or the anticipation of receiving rewards in heaven, but we bring the greatest glory to God when we obey and serve Him because we long to do what brings Him delight.

I was an excellent student because I had a burning desire to please my teachers. I did my homework on time and raised my hand before I spoke. This led to great satisfaction when my teacher would write on my paper, "100— Good Work!"

Many times Jesus put His own desire aside and chose to please God. Jesus prayed, "Not My will, but Thine be done." His greatest motive was His desire to please His Father. That's a great incentive for us, too.

Prayer

Father God, I have a longing to serve You. Let me put aside my desires and look to see what pleases You. I want to walk in a manner worthy of You. Amen.

Action

Do something today to intentionally honor God.

More Than "Just a Mom"

One generation shall praise Your works to another,
And shall declare Your mighty acts.

—PSALM 145:4

*M*any times as I presented my "More Hours in My Day" seminars around the country, I had the great opportunity to sign my books and chat with the women one-on-one. As we talked, some would tell me, "I'm just a mom" or "I'm just a housewife."

In the blink of an eye I would admonish them that they were more than just a mom or a housewife.

The secular world tries to give monetary value to the worth of a mom. Some have figured out that if you paid Mom comparable working wages, it would add up to at least 24,000 to 30,000 dollars a year.

But do we really see dollar signs when we're serving our loved ones? Hardly! We can't and don't charge money to our husbands and our children for loving them.

Being a mom and a housewife is the greatest calling a woman can have. As the home goes, so goes the world. You play an extremely valuable part in determining the future of our country. There can't be enough praises given to you.

I stand amazed at how much women love their families. You are an awesome breed. Don't ever be discouraged. Hold your head up high and know that you are obeying a sacred calling as a mother.

Prayer

Father God, thanks for calling me to being a mom. I ask that You never let me lose sight of who I am in Your eyes. Even if the world doesn't give me honor, I know that You do. Amen.

Action

Make the time to do what you need to make your life as a mom what you want it to be.

Seek His Thoughts

"For My thoughts are not your thoughts,
Nor are your ways My ways," declares the LORD.

—ISAIAH 55:8

Suppose a man should find a great basket by the wayside, carefully packed, and upon opening it he should find it filled with human thoughts—all the thoughts which had passed through one single brain in one year or five years. What a medley they would make! How many thoughts would be wild and foolish, how many weak and contemptible, how many mean and vile, how many so contradictory and crooked that they could hardly lie still in the basket. And suppose he should be told that these were all his own thoughts, children of his own brain; how amazed he would be, and how little prepared to see himself as revealed in those thoughts! How he would want to run away and hide, if all the world were to see the basket opened and see his thoughts.[15]

*W*ould your thoughts be an embarrassment to you?
I know that many of mine would be. Compared to the thoughts of God, we humans seem so frail. I can't imagine being exposed for the lowliness of my thoughts. I'm sometimes amazed that I could even think of such things—and

I certainly wouldn't want them revealed to the public. At times I want to crawl inside God's mind and see how it functions and how He thinks. Then I realize that He is the potter and I am the clay. His thoughts are much higher than mine.

In Philippians 4:8, Paul gives us some idea of God's level of thought process. He tells us to think on these things:

> Whatever is true
> Whatever is honorable
> Whatever is right
> Whatever is pure
> Whatever is of good report

As Christians we are all models that people watch to see what God is like. They are watching and listening to what we have to say about life. Either they accept our level of thought or they reject it by what they have learned, received, heard, and seen in us. Accordingly, we want to be the reflection of God to other people.

If people were to find your "thought basket" on the wayside, what kind of flowers would they pull out?

Prayer

Father God, may I continue to upgrade my thoughts so they will be more reflective of Your thoughts. May You help me to purge them so they stand the test of Your kind of thoughts. Amen.

Action

Evaluate your thought life. What do you see?

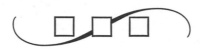

Knowing God in Stillness

Be still, and know that I am God....

—PSALM 46:10 (NKJV)

Last night my Bob and I watched the Grammy awards on television. This affair recognizes the best in a variety of music categories. At the end of the evening we both looked at each other and agreed, "We don't get it—most of this music is nothing but loud, loud sounds with words you can't hear or understand." A far cry from the music we grew up with.

We actually felt sorry for this current generation who has to listen to such noise. No wonder we live in an era where people are nervous, have short attention spans, have hearing problems, and have a difficult time being still. We are a culture that is severely overstimulated.

Do we even bother to listen for stillness, quietness, and silence anymore?

Yes, each of these do have a sound and it is so refreshing. For some people who have become addicted to noise, these sounds are uncomfortable. They become uneasy, nervous, twitching; they need sounds—loud sounds.

But quiet times are refreshing to the soul, offering us reflection, perhaps a chance to mourn or to be happy or maybe even to hear God speak to us in a still, small voice.

Do such times exist in your home? Or is your house filled with the discordant sounds of television and pop music? Is it any wonder then that you and your children don't know how to cultivate silence?

Perhaps your children are already well on the road to the addiction to noise—the need for constant audio activity. If so, you will be shortchanging them by not teaching them the joys of pure silence.

The psalmist knew that in order to know God we have to stop striving and become still. The business of life must come to a halt in order to know God. When we find ourselves with a hectic schedule and we're not sure we can get everything done, that is the moment to call "time-out" and seek the quietness that God can give us. Even a stillness of 60 to 90 seconds can restore your sense of direction. It doesn't take long.

Prayer

Father God, I find myself anxious; help me establish a quiet time each day so I can be still. In this stillness let me ponder who You are and may I know You in a greater way. Help me to establish my home as a place of peace, not audio discord. Amen.

Action

Tonight read a book or story to your children and ask them to experience two full minutes of silence. See if they can do it without squirming.

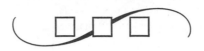

Encamped and Rescued

The angel of the LORD encamps around those
who fear Him, and rescues them.

—PSALM 34:7

$\mathscr{A}$s a child, did you ever build a clubhouse or a fort? Did you ever cover a table with blankets or towels and crawl inside to a safe, cozy nest?

That's what Psalm 34 reminds me of. The word "encamps" denotes making a camp or a fortress for protection—and that's what the Lord has done for each of us. I can feel it—can't you? Truly the Lord has given each of us our own special angel who wraps loving arms around us and delivers us from all harm.

I make it my practice to stand on this promise that no matter what happens, all's well. I believe the Lord will deliver me from current danger in His time and in His way, and that in the meantime He's keeping a close protective watch on me.

I continually feel His presence. He is always near, even when I feel I have moved away. He will never forsake us.

Harriet Beecher Stowe once said, "When you get in a tight place and everything goes against you, till it seems you could not hold on a minute longer, never give up then, for that is just the place and time that the tide will turn."

Prayer

Father God, You are my protector. You keep me safe when I need a shelter. When You are standing next to me, I feel so secure. Thanks for being my rock and foundation. Amen.

Action

Be brave enough to call on God when you aren't able to cope with your life.

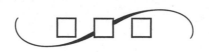

First Things First

Serve [worship] the LORD with gladness;
Come before Him with joyful singing.

—PSALM 100:2

*L*iving in this twenty-first century, we have so many activities to distract us that weren't available to our ancestors. We also have much more leisure time in which to pursue these activities.

In our neighborhood we constantly see people out for walks, jogging, playing in the park, heading for the mall, or, in the case of kids, skateboarding. Even the man of the house can be preoccupied with a full day of sports on the tube. All these are fun things to do, but they also present a danger when they prevent us from worshiping the Lord on Sunday.

Everyone loves the weekend. These are two days when we get to choose what we want to do. For many, the activities are errands they didn't accomplish during the week—grocery shopping, washing the car, doing laundry, cleaning the house, and so on. For others, Saturday and Sunday provide a break from a hard week on the job, a great time to relax.

Yes, weekends are fun to look forward to.

Unfortunately, worship doesn't always fit into our busy weekend schedule. Because of changing values in America, attendance at our church of choice is becoming a lower and lower weekend priority for many.

But you, Mom, can help your family recognize and heed this important weekly commitment of corporate worship. Rest assured, your children will notice the place of importance (or unimportance) Mom and Dad put on worshiping God. If they see that on a busy weekend, God is the first one cut out of the scheduled activities, the message they'll receive is that God is really a pretty low priority. That observation will translate into an even lesser commitment to God on their part.

But when we moms (and dads) are faithful to being a vital part of a good local church, the kids will notice and build a similar commitment into their own lives.

The opportunity to worship God with gladness is a freedom we too often take for granted. Being at church on the weekend is a divine appointment we must strive to keep. The weekend affords us plenty of hours to do the other things we want to do, without having to skip church.

There's simply nothing to compare with a family who delights in attending church together—filling the sanctuary with our presence, our songs of praise, our tithes and offerings, and with our joy in hearing God's Word preached.

Prayer

Father God, thank You for reminding me that my family is to worship You with gladness. We get so busy that we often forget what's really important. May our family be faithful in the matter of honoring You on the Lord's Day. Amen.

Action

Begin preparing your spirit for worshiping the Lord with gladness this weekend. Be excited when the Lord's Day arrives.

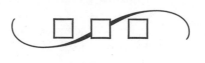

W. W. J. D.

For you have been called for this purpose,
since Christ also suffered for you,
leaving you an example for you to follow in His steps.

—1 PETER 2:21

Many years ago I read Charles M. Sheldon's book *In His Steps,* the story of a man who made a conscious effort to walk in the steps of Jesus. Before saying anything, doing anything, going anywhere, or making any decisions, he asked himself, "What would Jesus do?" Although living like Jesus was nearly impossible, this experience changed the man's life forever.

During our time on earth, daily situations will reveal our true character—but will our character point others toward Jesus? We do well to look to Jesus and His example of a godly life. He showed us how to live with kindness, gentleness, sympathy, and affection. He was always loving, forgiving, merciful, and patient. He had a strong sense of justice and compassion for the suffering and persecuted, and He willingly took a stand for what was right in God's eyes.

Jesus also knows all our pain and grief and our tragedy when friends betray us. He knows how hard it is to live in a world full of sickness and sin about which we can do very little. But what we can do—and this is following in Jesus' footsteps—is bring people to Him, the One who forgives, heals, and helps.

We can also let God work in our own hearts and lives so that He can make us more Christlike—and that's certainly something the world needs today.

No, we can never be exactly like Jesus. Our humanness and sin get in the way. But we can develop a teachable spirit. We can love God with all our hearts, minds, and strength. We can let Him transform us into more selfless, joyful women so that our character will reveal the likeness of Jesus.

As Jesus' representatives in the world today, we walk in His steps when we help the helpless, pray for the sick, feed and clothe the homeless, and support those whom God lifts up to minister in places we haven't been called to go.

In our mothering, we can see our children through the eyes of Him who said to His people, "How often I wanted to gather your children together, the way a hen gathers her chicks under her wings, and you were unwilling" (Matthew 23:37).

Prayer

Father God, grant me today a new revelation. Help me step out and trust You in a new way. I want to see people as You see them. Amen.

Action

Walk in Jesus' steps today. Do something that would be Christlike. Teach your children about WWJD. If possible, visit your local Christian bookstore and buy each family member one of those inexpensive woven bracelets with the letters WWJD on them.

What Has the Locust Eaten of Yours?

...I will make up to you for the years that the swarming locust has eaten...you will have plenty to eat and be satisfied and praise the name of the LORD your God....

—JOEL 2:25-26

Historically, farmers throughout the world have had to contend with losing their crops to the gnawing, crawling, and consuming locust. One's whole work for a year can be quickly destroyed when the locusts swoop down to devour everything in their path. Wealth has turned to bankruptcy through the actions of the locust.

In America, rural farmers were devastated by the invasion of this swarming locust. Farmers have had to move hundreds of miles and even find a new line of work because the locust knocked their legs from under them.

But God is a God of restoration! Even when the devastation to a human life is as thorough as the work of a swarm of locusts on a promising crop—even then, God promises to restore completely everything that has been destroyed. In today's verse, He says His people will have plenty to eat, will be satisfied, and will be able to praise God. Wow, what a wonderful picture of the thoroughness of God's restorative power!

What have the locusts eaten of yours? A job, a child, a reputation, a husband, a friend? We all have had losses due to locusts in our lives. Perhaps some of you have already seen God's restoration and are rejoicing. But others of you may still be looking out over fields that were once full and rich with bounty—now destroyed.

The locusts have beaten you down. Your energy has been sapped—you are no longer joyful. You wonder if life can ever be the same again.

Look up! Your fields can be restored. Your Savior's promise for Israel can also be claimed for your life. No matter what the locusts have stripped from you, you can be restored.

Yes, you can even praise God for the locusts of the past. Their devastation is simply a pathway for God to move— and when God moves to restore, He does a great job! Just ask Job.

God renews our past by renewing our present. He gives us new peace, new joy, new goals, new dreams, and new love. Your present situation can overshadow the discouragement of the past. *What God has promised He will do.*

Prayer

Father God, thank You for my promised restoration. I look to You to give back all that was so quickly and horribly lost. I trust You and look forward to each new day that You will work restoration in my life— and that of my family. Amen.

Action

Let God restore the locusts' damage in your life.

Glass Half-Full

O Lord, I am oppressed, be my security.
—ISAIAH 38:14

As a busy mom, perhaps you wake up "oppressed." I know that I often did. Young moms are always tired in the morning. They never get enough sleep. They arise to children who demand attention, a husband who needs help out the door, breakfast that needs preparation, a house that begs for cleaning…and then there are the unexpected monkey wrenches that seem to arrive at the worst time. The sick child, the spilled milk, the husband's car that won't start—so, now he'll have to take your car, leaving you unable to do all those errands you'd planned.

Yes, Mom, I remember those days when I felt oppressed by such events.

At such times, all I could do was cry out to God, "Lord, undertake for me; I'm not able to handle all that needs to be done." Then invariably, when I took a deep breath, calmed my spirit, and sought counsel, I was able to pick up the pieces and get past this stint of oppression.

David in the book of Psalms was a great model of how to get over oppression. None of us will ever endure what he had to overcome, but here was a biblical character who took daily oppressions and made them into victories. A few minutes spent reading in the book of Psalms has the power to remove even the strongest oppression and set you quickly back on track.

Prayer

Father God, let my spirit pause and relax as I feel so overwhelmed with what needs to be done today. You are my victory for today's oppressions. Amen.

Action

Make lemonade out of a lemon. Make sure that all your glasses are half-full, not half-empty.

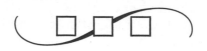

Cease from Worry

And who of you by being worried
can add a single hour to his life?

—MATTHEW 6:27

Oh, do we like to worry. We worry about everything.

> Will there be enough money to pay our bills?
> Will the children stay out of trouble?
> Does my husband love me?
> Why don't I have more friends?
> Am I a good homemaker?
> Is my husband's job secure or will he be getting
>   laid off?

Eighty-five percent of the things we worry about never happen. We tire ourselves out by trying to use our positive energy on negative issues. Stop worrying and begin to resolve our concerns with positive endeavors. Concentrate on those issues that we can do something about.

Pray more.

Read more.

Love more.

Be more organized.

Take a cooking class.

Become a friend.

Stop thinking negatively and sing a new song. Let God know that you are trusting in Him to give you clear direction in your life. Don't get caught up in an ulcer-producing and peace-destroying lifestyle. Worry is not God's best for us. When we worry, it doesn't keep bad things from happening. It just prevents us from enjoying the good things of life.

Prayer

Father God, today I want to stop worrying. Let me be brave with this decision. Let me move forward with the assurance that You will handle my every need. Amen.

Action

Write down five blessings on a piece of paper. Look at this list at least once each day for five days.

He Is My Shepherd

The LORD is…

—PSALM 23:1

*I*n his most beautiful psalm of trust, David pictures the Lord as the great Shepherd who provides for and protects His sheep and as the gracious Host who protects and provides abundantly for His guests.

At the very beginning of this great psalm we read, "The Lord is…"

That's all we need to know. The Lord IS!! He is all we need. We don't need any other. He is the hub of our life. All else revolves around Him. He is what makes sense out of this crazy world.

When my good health was disrupted by cancer, I started each new day with this proclamation, "The Lord is." He is my supporter, my courage, my encourager, my trust, my salvation, and my purpose. He is the beginning and the end. Nothing else matters but Jesus. He is the rock of my foundation. He is the hearer and responder to my prayers.

At times I haven't even known how to pray, but I know that the Holy Spirit intercedes for me.

My whole purpose in life only matters as it revolves around my relationship to my Lord. The Lord is everything!

He is everything for you too, Mom. Always remember that.

Prayer

Father God, may I never forget to call on You in every situation. I want to call on You every day of my life. Thank You for being within the sound of my voice and only a thought's distance away. Amen.

Action

Complete this sentence with whatever is appropriate for your need. The Lord is my _____.

Enter Into Thy Closet

...when you pray, go into your [inner] room,
and when you have shut your door,
pray to your Father who is in the secret place;
and your Father who sees in secret will reward you openly.

—MATTHEW 6:6 (NKJV)

What a privilege as moms to be able to have a "closet" in which to enter. Any private space will do. Just an area we can set apart where we can meet with God and pray, meditate, study, cry, or even laugh.

I have a wonderful friend in Arizona who recently remodeled her home and built a specific space for a prayer closet. It's decorated in detail just as you would furnish any room. It's carpeted, painted, has good lighting, shelving for books, Kleenex for tears, writing materials, and even a kneeling bench. Her family has agreed to respect the time Mom is in her "prayer closet." No interruptions for anything. The world stops when Donna is alone with God. As a result of her new special room, Donna tells me her time with God is richer than ever before—and I believe her.

One mother told me she used her kitchen apron to put over her head when she needed to be alone with God. Her family knew that when Mom had her head covered she wasn't to be disturbed. A prayer closet can be as simple as that apron over the head, or a room built especially for prayer—but in any event, wherever your closet is, *enter it.*

Prayer

Father God, give me a place where I can be alone with You. I desire this precious time alone away from the hustle and bustle of the day. Amen.

Action

Establish a special place of prayer—a prayer "closet," and enter it.

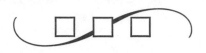

Weeping Comes at Night

Woman, why are you weeping?

—JOHN 20:15

Oh, fellow mom, if only you could hear the stories that my pillowcase could tell you. I've cried so many tears. As a young child of 11, I had tears of sadness when my dad passed away, leaving me fatherless. As a young mother, I cried over lost dreams, my lack of energy, my responsibilities, and the death of my mother. Recently I've cried a lot when told by my doctor that I had cancer. There's something about tragedy and the limits of our precious life that lead to tears.

Sometimes we moms just need to cry. As women we need the healthy release tears bring. At these times, Bob will ask me what's wrong. I will honestly tell him I feel like crying. Naturally, being a man, he doesn't always understand why I cry.

Tears will be part of our life experience. Welcome them when they come. They help clear out our emotional and physical systems. As an added bonus, Jesus will take all your tears and make them into rays of sunlight.

One of my most encouraging verses is found in Psalm 30:5:

Weeping may last for the night,
But a shout of joy comes in the morning.

Prayer

Father God, thank You for letting me weep. My soul reaches out in tender care to my family, to the helpless, to the victims of crime, and to all who are hurting. Thank You for the gift of tears. May they accomplish their every purpose in my life. Amen.

Action

Be encouraged, not discouraged, when you weep.

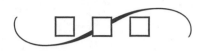

Let's Not Get Weary

God is our refuge and strength,
A very present help in trouble.

—Psalm 46:1

*D*o you ever feel like throwing in the towel and walking away from it all? Does motherhood sometimes feel over-bearing—even impossible? Is the world becoming too complex to keep a balance? Many times throughout my life I've thought, *What's the use?*

One of my friends told about an experience she had with her daughter after she had corrected her for some inappropriate behavior. The daughter quickly replied, "Gosh, Mom, do I have to act decent all the time?" This young girl had already caught the sentiments of the time—she was growing weary.

Sometimes women will ask if I get tired of what I do. I answer truthfully, "Yes, I do get tired." I think we all get tired of our daily tasks, frequent demands on our time, meeting obligations we may not like to do.

At times, we all get tired of being "decent."

But moms, let's not lose hope in our calling. Let's look beyond our tiredness to the rewards of being faithful as a mother. Who we are and what we do makes all the difference in the world to those around us. At times it may not seem like it, but we determine the future for those we love.

Get tired but not weary. And believe me, to *not* fulfill our missions as mothers will result in an even more debilitating tiredness as we watch our children suffer from our failure to be the mom they need.

Prayer

Father God, let me work, get tired, and take refuge in You my strength. When I don't feel like going on, give me my second breath to run the race of life. Amen.

Action

Be an encouragement to some weary person. New energy (both emotional and physical) comes when we give to others.

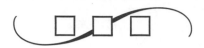

Love Never Fails

Love never fails.

—1 Corinthians 13:8

*I*n this great love chapter (1 Corinthians 13), we are taught the attributes of love. They are: love is patient, love is kind, love is not jealous, love does not brag, love is not arrogant, love does not act unbecomingly, love does not seek its own, love does not provoke, love does not keep record of wrongs, love does not get happy over wrongdoings, love gets excited about truth, love becomes all things, love believes all things, love endures all things, and love never fails.

As our culture becomes more and more impersonal, we need to be sensitive to the devices that separate us from the real emotions of life. Computers, the Internet, earphones, sitcoms, pulp fiction, and the music of modern culture all make us callous to the real experience of godly love. They are at war with our ability to love rightly.

Real love can be frightening. We take risks when we love. It may not be easy. We often have to work at love. We have to learn to listen, to cry, to laugh, to experience it.

But in spite of all this: Mom, take time to learn to love, because love never fails.

Prayer

Father God, let me be a woman of love. I want Your spirit to flow through my every expression to those around me. Let my friends know that I truly love them. Amen.

Action

Go out and really show love to those you meet today.

Be on the Alert

*...be on the alert—for you do not know
when the master of the house is coming....*

—MARK 13:35

I know as a busy mom I was always on the alert. I watched for everything: the mood of the family, coupons for savings at the market, what time the children came home at night, what friends they hung out with.

Moms are more intuitively alert to the family than most dads. Bob would often come to me and ask how things were going with the children. He knew that I was more alert to what was happening.

The Scripture tells us to stay on the alert as doorkeepers of our homes. The world creeps in so subtly that we often don't recognize when it knocks at our doors.

One of our favorite verses is in Romans 12:2: "And do not be conformed to this world, but be transformed by the renewing of your mind, so that you may prove what the will of God is, that which is good and acceptable and perfect." We call it "conformed versus transformed."

Be alert until the day Jesus comes. We don't know the day or the hour of His return. Be ready.

Prayer

Father God, I sometimes let my guard down and become complacent to the world. Help me not to take for granted that all's well with my family or to be aggravated by this reminder to "be alert." Amen.

Action

Take special note of your children's friends. Any red flags?

Choose to Be Strong

My help comes from the LORD,
Who made heaven and earth.

—PSALM 121:2

$\mathcal{A}$s I have walked through my cancer diagnosis and treatment these last few years, I've often wondered if I am going to make it. Yes, my support group encouraged me, and hundreds and hundreds of prayer partners assured me by cards and letters that I was going to make it, but my mind was often plagued with negative thoughts about my future. Satan so wanted to defeat me by making me lose hope for recovery. Yet my faith remained victorious and my daily walk with God helped me climb the many mountains put before me.

Bill Martin, Jr. tells a story of how a young Indian boy was able to overcome his fear of failure:

"Grandfather, will I ever be strong like you?" the little boy asked. His grandfather reassured him, "You're growing stronger every day."

"How strong must I be, Grandfather?" the boy asked.

"You must be so strong that you will not speak with anger, even when your heart is filled with anger....You must be so strong that you will listen to what others are saying, even when your own thoughts are begging for expression....You must be so strong that you will always stop to remember what happened yesterday and foresee what will happen tomorrow so that you will know what to do today."

"Then will I be strong enough to cross over the dark mountains?" the boy asked.

The wise grandfather answered, "You already have crossed some of the dark mountains, my grandson. But these mountains of sorrow have no beginning and no ending. They are all around us. We can only know that we are crossing them when we want to be weak but choose to be strong."

Mom, when you're called to cross the dark mountains surrounding you, be brave, even when you feel like being weak. Lift your face skyward and pray that God will give you strength far beyond your expectations.

Prayer

Father God, when I am weak, then am I strong. When I don't feel like going on, push me out of my comfort zone and let me face the unknown knowing that You are beside me every step of the way. Be my solid rock. Amen.

Action

Sing or speak the words to the great hymn of the faith "The Solid Rock."

My hope is built on nothing less
Than Jesus' blood and righteousness.
I dare not trust the sweetest frame,
But wholly lean on Jesus' Name.

On Christ the solid Rock I stand,
All other ground is sinking sand;
All other ground is sinking sand.

When darkness seems to hide His face,
I rest on His unchanging grace.
In every high and stormy gale,
My anchor holds within the veil.

On Christ the solid Rock I stand,
All other ground is sinking sand;
All other ground is sinking sand.

His oath, His covenant, His blood,
Support me in the whelming flood.
When all around my soul gives way,
He then is all my Hope and Stay.

On Christ the solid Rock I stand,
All other ground is sinking sand;
All other ground is sinking sand.

When He shall come with trumpet sound,
Oh may I then in Him be found.
Dressed in His righteousness alone,
Faultless to stand before the throne.

On Christ the solid Rock I stand,
All other ground is sinking sand;
All other ground is sinking sand.

Change Is a Gift

...we will not all sleep, but we will all be changed....
—1 CORINTHIANS 15:51

$\mathscr{I}$ have had the privilege of undergoing many changes in my life. During each episode I've learned a lot about who I really am. The changes, in fact, have helped *make* me who I am.

Even with my recent change—the diagnosis of cancer—I can say it has been a gift of God to help shape me into the woman He's called me to be. In addition, I've met so many wonderful people whom I would not have met if I had not been faced with this illness.

The many changes in my life have left it hard for me to imagine living a lifetime doing the same thing year after year.

Several years ago we had the opportunity to visit a church which we had attended 30 years before. As we walked into the sanctuary, we were shocked to see that many of the people we had known 30 years before were sitting in the same pews they had sat in when we were members. The only difference was that these people were 30 years older, but they were still doing the same thing they had always done.

Don't get me wrong: I'm all for tradition, family, and stability, but I'm also into being open to God and seeing the new horizons He's planned for me.

Suppose tonight your husband walks through the door and announces that he has been offered a promotion and transfer to another city. What would your response be? Would you be angry, unsettled, worried? Or would you jump with joy, realizing that change is a gift from God. Your husband's promotion is, in a real way, *your* promotion, too. God is moving you on to something new and exciting. There are good people He wants you to meet, a fine church He would like you to attend, and a new home He wants you to establish.

Mom, look *forward* to see what God will do to your life in this change. Anticipate change as you remember with fondness the gifts God has given you in the past.

Prayer

Father God, thanks for letting me see change in a positive manner. I welcome any change You might give me. Amen.

Action

Don't merely accept change, anticipate it.

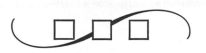

Garage Sales Are Fun

I would rather stand at the threshold of the house of my God,
Than dwell in the tents of wickedness.

—PSALM 84:10

*W*e have just put on the biggest garage sale of our lives. In fact it was so big and of such great interest in our community we called it "Emilie Barnes' Estate Sale."

After living 15 years at the "Barnes' Barn," we needed to move closer to my oncologist 45 miles away. In preparation for the move, we had to go through everything and sort what to keep, sell, give away, or throw away.

It wasn't all that easy. We had to make some hard decisions on what was important. We had spent more than 40 years accumulating nice things for our home. As a result, visitors to our home often expressed how warm and comfortable they felt. My efforts at creating a "home" also resulted in our house being featured in several home and garden magazines and books over the years.

Our sorting experience brought to mind another couple who also held a garage sale because they were moving to a smaller home. One of their possessions was a book of sayings this couple had collected that reflected their thoughts about life. One section was called "We Leave Our Children." It reads:

We leave our children...
The most precious of all gifts—familial, brotherly,
and spiritual;

our attention, for one day they may not hear us
a value system
self-reliance, courage, conviction, and respect for
    self and others
a sense of humor—for laughter is life's gyro
discipline—else life will be a bitter teacher
a will to work—for work well done brings pride
    and joy
a talent for sharing—for society needs belief in
    individual worth
the passion of truth—for truth is a straight answer,
the beginning of trust
the lantern of hope—which lights the dark corners
    of the mind
the knowledge of belonging
impromptu praise
a soft caress
a sense of wonder at the things of nature
a love of friends without reciprocity
the size of God's Word, in print so small it fits
    inside each heart, in meaning so great it spreads
    over the earth

This wise couple left their children far more than a monetary legacy. They left love.

Prayer

Father God, in life we must sort out what to keep,
sell, or give away. Give me the wisdom to know
what's important in life. Amen.

Action

Have a garage sale of your mind—weed out what to
keep and what to give away.

Praying for Myself as a Wife

Make me my husband's helpmate, companion, champion, friend, and support. Help me to create a peaceful, restful, safe place for him to come home to. Teach me how to take care of myself and stay attractive to him. Grow me into a creative and confident woman who is rich in mind, soul, and spirit. Make me the kind of woman he can be proud to say is his wife.

I lay all my expectations at Your cross. I release my husband from the burden of fulfilling me in areas where I should be looking to You. Help me to accept him the way he is and not try to change him....I leave any changing that needs to be done in Your hands, fully accepting that neither of us is perfect and never will be. Only You, Lord, are perfect and I look to You to perfect us.

Teach me how to pray for my husband and make my prayers a true language of love.[16]

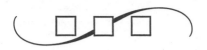

Words Have Power

For as he thinks within himself, so he is.

—Proverbs 23:7

An English professor once said, "Develop a rich vocabulary, for without the right language, the soul is impoverished." This man was correct. Words shape our thoughts, thoughts shape our attitudes, and attitudes shape our will.

From junior and senior high school, I can remember several English teachers who stressed the importance of thinking before speaking. They also promoted vocabulary development in their students and a love for the written word.

As women of God we need to be disciplined in the words we use. Not only is this proper, but it also determines who we are and whom we are becoming. Let's not limit ourselves by not being able to express ourselves properly.

When we discipline our use of words, we allow God to fill our minds with wholesome thoughts that influence our destiny. Paul in Philippians 4:8 gives us some insight on how we can improve our thought process. He says, "Finally, brethren, whatever is true, whatever is honorable, whatever is right, whatever is pure, whatever is lovely, whatever is of good repute, if there is any excellence and if anything worthy of praise, dwell on these things."

Prayer

Father God, I have found proper words to be so powerful. I want continually to learn something new each day. Help me be the disciplined mom I want to be. Amen.

Action

Discard all negative thoughts today.

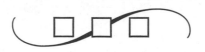

Cleaning Turns Me On

*...For you are like whitewashed tombs which
on the outside appear beautiful, but inside they are full
of dead men's bones and all uncleanness.*

—MATTHEW 23:27

As you may know, I'm into cleaning. My Bob says he knows when I'm feeling good, because I have a rake and feather duster in my hands. When my little nest is clean, I feel so good. Pine-Sol is one of my very best friends.

I get really excited about cleaning out closets. I know I feel good after cleaning out a messy closet, but I'm not sure the closet feels any better—just emptier.

One day as I was cleaning out my front closet, I found a great many things I hadn't used in years. I even came upon lost Christmas gifts from a few years back.

Usually I prefer to clean by myself—no one around. At such times, I can get into really deep thought. Sometimes I think God speaks to me as I clean.

The other day when I was rearranging clutter in one of the bedrooms, I started rethinking about some burdens I'd been shelving internally, many of which I'd forgotten about—sort of like those lost Christmas presents.

Then I realized those burdens were like dead men's bones cluttering my mind. I realized I needed to dust off my thoughts, clean out the closet of my mind, and banish those burdens to the trash bin forever.

As I dusted off my mental cobwebs, I gave my burdens to the Lord. He took my cobwebs, my burdens, and helped me receive forgiveness for all those skeletons I had stored away for so long.

Moms, God can clean out your old ways of thinking, too. Don't you think it's time for a little mental and spiritual cleaning of the closets?

Prayer

Father God, take all the clatter and clutter out of my mind and replace them with peace. Make room for pleasant thoughts as You remove the cobwebs of worry and remorse. Help me know which thoughts are worth keeping and which must go. Amen.

Action

Clean out one of your closets. Have three trash bags to put your contents into. They are: give away, throw away, and put away. While the closet is empty, clean it good. You might even want to repaint.

If It Is God's Will

*...you ought to say, "If the Lord wills,
we will live and also do this or that."*

—James 4:15

*O*ne thing I've learned is that life is very uncertain. We can say we will do this or that, but we can't know for sure that it will happen.

I've had to change so many of my plans, because of illness, change of mind, change of priorities, or because God simply intervenes and rearranges everything.

That doesn't mean I've become negative or that I've lost hope along the way. No, it means that I've begun to realize that God has a master plan behind all of His mysteries. I've begun to realize that only God knows what the future holds.

Lately, one of my emphases has been found in the Lord's Prayer (Matthew 6:6-13), when it says, "Our Father which art in heaven, Hallowed be thy name. Thy kingdom come. Thy will be done..." (KJV).

Yes, *Thy* will be done. After all these years, I am still learning to accept and praise God for letting "Thy will be done" in my life.

Mom, your life is different than mine. You have different opportunities and different challenges. But as believers in Christ, we can rest assured that He has the very best in mind for our lives. In today's Scripture reading, James is saying:

* Let God be first in your life. Make Him number one.
* Realize that whatever comes, comes from God. We are nothing without Him.
* In all that you have and do, do it all to the glory of God.

Prayer

Father God, You are a holy God. One who loves and cares for me. You light my path so I will not stumble. Guide me into this wisdom, "Thy will be done" in my life. Amen.

Action

Realize that God has a plan for your life and always affirm your plans by adding, "If the Lord wills."

Work Is a Gift

...God has given riches and wealth, He has also empowered him to eat from them and to receive his reward and rejoice in his labor; this is the gift of God.

—ECCLESIASTES 5:19

In the olden days, a man or woman's work was perceived as God's blessing; people would do their work "as unto the Lord." In studying history we find the great musicians, sculptors, painters, and craftsmen all creating works reflecting their love for God.

Today we seem to have lost that tremendous concept. Many people consider work as a curse, a penalty, or a burden. These people usually struggle out of bed in the morning to go to that boring job or begin the drudgery of their housework. They live for the weekend instead of appreciating the gift of their daily work.

We all would be a lot happier—and much better workers—if we recaptured the idea that our work, our wealth, and our possessions are all gifts from God, and we can thank Him by doing our very best at our jobs.

As Christian moms we should be the best workers in our homes, streets, or companies. We should be the best moms for our children that we can be.

We must realize that a mother's work is a gift from God.

Prayer

Father God, I want to change my attitude to that of being thankful for my work. I want to see my love for You manifest in my daily responsibilities. May those around me see You by my work. Amen.

Action

Let all your work reflect your love for God.

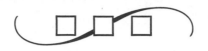

Let Your Face Shine

*...A man's wisdom illumines him
and causes his stern face to beam.*

—ECCLESIASTES 8:1

Let us make one point...that we meet each other with
a smile, when it is difficult to smile.... Smile at each
other, make time for each other in your family.

—MOTHER TERESA

Wherever I go, a smile is the common denominator for
happiness. I have never turned down a smile sent in my
direction, nor have I become angry at anyone who smiles
back to me. To me, a smile is a profound blessing one
person can give another. It costs the giver very little, and
the receiver takes away a beautiful, unexpected gift. You'll
never know when your smile is the only smile a person will
receive that day.

You've probably heard that it takes more muscles to
frown than to smile. That's true—but a smile does take
some effort. It takes wisdom enough to notice another
person and choose to connect with him or her to share a
little something from the heart. A smile might not be
returned—but it's never wasted. Shared blessings never
are!

Perhaps the most important recipient of one of your smiles today will be one of your children. Let them see you smile their way often. Teach them the value of a smile and the rewards of being friendly. Someday when you're gone, it will be nice to think that they will say of you, "I remember the wonderful way my mother had of smiling. I miss her smiles immensely."

Prayer

Father God, let me receive all the smiles that are given to me today. I will consider each a blessing from You. May I also give my smiles freely to others today, especially my children. Amen.

Action

Smile at everyone you meet today. Give them one of your blessings.

Be Observant

Blessed be the Lord,
Who daily loads us with benefits,
The God of our salvation!

—PSALM 68:19 (NKJV)

I never can understand people when they can't get excited about life. It amazes me that some people find life dull and boring. They must not be seeing and hearing the same life that I do.

All one has to do is look around and observe, watch, look, and listen. Everything in sight is in some way a blessing from God. Honestly, He is daily giving me more blessings than I can receive—truly my cup overflows.

When I realize that the ray of sunlight I see is there for me, I say, "Thank You." When the trees wave their branches, I say, "Thank You, Lord." The birds that sing, the fruits, the vegetables, and the blooming flowers are also just for me, and I say, "Thank You."

Everything from the smiles we receive, the hand extended, the hugs that warm us, and the compliments that enter our ears are all blessings from God. I can't help but be overjoyed by the stimulation He sends my way.

I can't help but count these as blessing, too: the food we eat, the air we breathe, the jobs we have, the family God gives us, friendly neighbors—these are all part of the daily benefits given by God. And all that people have to do to receive these is open their senses to find this exciting life. God is so good every day.

Prayer

Father God, don't let me take anything for granted. Let me open my eyes each day and take in all the benefits You have given me. Let me slow down and smell the roses. Each day You give me so many benefits. Amen.

Action

Open your eyes and see God's benefits. Teach your children to love life and to be thankful.

Great Is Thy Faithfulness

*The LORD's lovingkindnesses indeed never cease
For His compassions never fail.
They are new every morning;
Great is Your faithfulness.*

—LAMENTATIONS 3:22-23

*I*n 1923, Thomas O. Chisholm and William M. Runyan put these words from Lamentations to music. In the decades since, it has become one of the great hymns of the church. The words are

Great is Thy faithfulness, O God my Father!
There is no shadow of turning with Thee.
Thou changest not, Thy compassions, they fail not;
As Thou hast been Thou forever wilt be.

Summer and winter, and springtime and harvest,
Sun, moon, and stars in their courses above,
Join with all nature in manifold witness,
To Thy great faithfulness, mercy, and love.

Pardon for sin and a peace that endureth,
Thy own dear presence to cheer and to guide,
Strength for today and bright hope for tomorrow—
Blessings all mine with ten thousand beside!

Chorus

Great is Thy faithfulness, Great is Thy faithfulness,
Morning by morning, new mercies I see;
All I have needed Thy hand hath provided
Great is Thy faithfulness, Lord unto me! Amen

Lamentations 3:22 tells us that the steadfast love of the Lord never ceases, His mercies never come to an end; they are new every morning.

The Lord is so good to those who wait for Him. The soul that seeks Him, shall find Him. Even though we are sinners, God has bestowed so much grace on us through His Son Jesus that we can wake each morning afresh. We have been forgiven and we are as white as snow. The cross provided a second chance for us all. God is so faithful; all of life's joys and all of our happiness comes through what happened at the cross. His unselfish act has given me eternal life.

Prayer

Father God, I humbly thank You for being so faithful. I deserve death, but You gave me life. I appreciate the eternal life You give me each new day. Amen.

Action

Go out and praise God for His faithfulness to you and your family. Tonight as the family gathers for dinner, give each person a copy of the words to this great hymn and sing it as your dinner blessing.

Two Kinds of Wisdom

Who among you is wise and understanding? Let him show by his good behavior his deeds in the gentleness of wisdom.

—James 3:13

My husband Bob has an identical twin brother named Bill. When our children, Jennifer and Bradley, were very young, they couldn't tell them apart. When Bob and Bill were together, our children would say, "Two daddies." When our grandchildren arrived, they too were confused when we were all together. They would say, "Two papas."

That's the way it is with wisdom. There are two types of wisdom. They come from different sources, have different meanings, and most definitely have different ends. James talks about these two wisdoms in chapter 3, verses 15-18:

One comes from above
One is earthly, natural, and demonic

The one that comes from above is—
Pure
Gentle
Peaceable
Reasonable
Full of mercy
Full of good fruits
Unwavering

The second wisdom produces—
Bitter jealousy
Selfish ambition
Lies against the truth
Arrogance

Notice the difference in the fruit that each one
     produces—
The first produces the fruit of righteousness and peace.
The second produces the fruit of disorder and every
     evil thing.

Some young Christians have trouble telling these twins apart. They might mistake one for the other. But, just like our kids learned to know which Daddy was theirs because of the love he had for them, so too can we learn to know the wisdom that sets us on the right path. As we spend time learning this heavenly wisdom, it becomes much more recognizable until we know it well, even from a distance.

Spend time with the true wisdom and you'll never mistake it for the false. Learn it while you're young...don't wait until you're old and can only see wisdom in hindsight.

Luci Swindoll says:

> The good life is peace—knowing that I was considerate instead of crabby, that I stood by faithfully when all the chips were down for the other guy, that I showed impartiality when I really wanted my preference, that I had the courage to deter reward for something better down the road. Why couldn't I have learned this when I still had a young body?

Prayer
     Father God, I would like to be the exception. I don't want to have to wait until I'm old to have wisdom. I also don't want to wait for the hard knocks and suffering in order to earn this prize called wisdom. Amen.

Action
     Be wise in the decisions you make today.

Notes

1. John W. Yates, III, "Pottering and Prayer," in *Christianity Today,* April 2, 2001, (Carol Stream, IL), p. 61 .

2. Elon Foster, editor, *6,000 Sermon Illustrations* (Grand Rapids, MI: Baker Book House, 1992), p. 639.

3. David Augsburger, *Sustaining Love* (Ventura, CA: Regal Books, 1988)

4. Emilie Barnes, *Emilie's Creative Home Organizer* (Eugene, OR: Harvest House Publishers, 1995), p. 224.

5. Nenien C. McPherson, Jr., quoted in Charles L. Wallis, *The Treasure Chest* (New York, NY: Harper Collins Publishers Inc., 1995), p. 20.

6. Colleen and Louise Evans, Jr., *My Lover, My Friend* (Old Tappan, NJ: Fleming H. Revell, 1976), pp. 121-23.

7. Dwight H. Small, *Christian: Celebrate Your Sexuality* (Old Tappan, NJ: Fleming H. Revell, 1974), p. 144.

8. June Masters Bacher, *Quiet Moments for Women* (Eugene, OR: Harvest House Publishers, 1979), February 3 reading.

9. H. Norman Wright, *Quiet Times for Couples* (Eugene, OR: Harvest House Publishers, 1990), p. 170.

10. Lloyd J. Ogilvie, *God's Best for My Life* (Eugene, OR: Harvest House Publishers, 1981), January 16th reading.

11. Bacher, *Quiet Moments for Women,* September 8 reading.

12. Quoted in Charles R. Swindoll, *Growing Strong in the Seasons of Life* (Portland, OR: Multnomah Press, 1983), p. 66.

13. Wright, *Quiet Times for Couples,* p. 18.

14. Augsburger, *Sustaining Love,* p. 101.

15. Foster, *6,000 Sermon Illustrations,* p. 627.

16. Stormie Omartian, excerpt from *The Power of a Praying® Wife* (Eugene, OR: Harvest House Publishers, 1997), pp. 13-23.

Other Harvest House Books
by Bob & Emilie Barnes

🐦 🐦 🐦

Books by
Bob & Emilie Barnes

*Minute Meditations
for Couples*

*A Little Book of Manners
for Boys*

Abundance of the Heart

*15 Minute Devotions
for Couples*

Books by Emilie Barnes

The 15-Minute Organizer

15 Minutes Alone with God

*15 Minutes of Peace
with God*

101 Ways to Lift Your Spirits

*The Busy Woman's Guide
to Healthy Eating*

A Tea to Comfort Your Soul

A Cup of God's Love

A Cup of Hope

A Different Kind of Miracle

*Emilie's Creative
Home Organizer*

*Everything I Know
I Learned from My Garden*

Fill My Cup, Lord

Friends Are a Blessing

Friends of the Heart

Help Me Trust You, Lord

If Teacups Could Talk

An Invitation to Tea

Join Me for Tea

*Keep It Simple
for Busy Women*

Let's Have a Tea Party!

A Little Book of Manners

*Minute Meditations
for Busy Moms*

*Minute Meditations
for Women*

More Hours in My Day

The Promise of Hope

Safe in the Father's Hands

*Strength for Today,
Bright Hope for Tomorrow*

Survival for Busy Women

The Twelve Teas™ of Christmas

*The Twelve Teas™
of Friendship*

Books by Bob Barnes

*15 Minutes Alone with God
for Men*

Minute Meditations for Men

*What Makes a Man
Feel Loved*